By Life or By Death

The Journey of a Martyr's Daughter

AVIS BODIN

with Vicki Buchhold

By Life or By Death

Cover design by Robert Ousnamer.

Cover background image used by permission, copyright: <a href='http://www.123rf.com/profile_mtilghma'>mtilghm a / 123RF Stock Photo</a>

ISBN-13: 978-1-941733-12-7

Published by EA Books, Inc.
www.eabooksonlinel.com

DEDICATION

To my mom, Audrey Bacon Hoogshagen. To all those who grew up in the mission field.

And to my beloved husband, Ron.

TABLE OF CONTENTS

FOREWORD

Avis and I attend the same church. We've worked together and shared moments of fellowship and friendship. Rarely do such relationships result in coming to know someone well. So much of our lives are put away and hidden from our present-day existence. We show what we want seen and say what we want heard. We wear our masks. Not that Avis isn't genuine in her actions and speech—quite the opposite is true. But I didn't really know her.

When she asked for my help in writing this story, I knew it was a story worth telling. What I didn't know was that her account of great loss and triumph teemed with adventure, danger, sadness, turmoil, humor, endurance, honesty, devotion, and boundless love. I didn't know the depth of a missionary's calling.

My own experience doesn't easily give way to the hard fact that there is more to faith than this comfortable road I've traveled. When I began the journey of writing *By Life or Death* I didn't know I would see and hear things far beyond my limited view of the Christian walk. I didn't know the masks would come off. I'm glad they did.

Vicki Buchhold

BOLIVIA
Santa Rosa
Rurrenabaque
The Beni
Santiago
Santa Corazon
Tobite
Porton
Robore
Santa Cruz
El Carmen
Arica
Chili
Corumba
Brazil
N
W
E
S
RB 4/18

CHAPTER 1
FIRST CONTACT

In1943 my father walked into the ominous green jungle in the lowlands of Bolivia with four other men. They left their rented houses, their wives and children with a single purpose. Seven entered the harsh land knowing they could back out of the trip. No one would judge them. Two walked out, back to civilization.

The group had encountered natives in the village of Santo Corazón without any trouble, but a tribe of Ayoré Indians lived deep in the jungle. My father and the others were the first to contact the ones who lived where white men had never been seen. They would learn how the secluded tribe lived, how they survived. An arduous task of gaining trust would begin. The Ayorés would meet a peaceful group. Unarmed, defenseless, my father walked into the jungle.

His name was David Bacon. My tiny, courageous, pregnant mother waited, watched from the door of the little whitewashed house that she shared with another anxious wife. I was the one unborn. The men had instructed the two who'd changed their minds: "If we don't come out in a month or two, come in and look for us."

My mother hoped and prayed it wouldn't be so long. But a month passed, then two. A search party was formed to travel the route the five had taken. They found a ripped piece of a boot, a page from a Bible, and my father's watch. They returned to the village. There was no sign that my father and the other men had been killed by the natives, but assumptions were made.

The searchers gave the watch to my mother—a timepiece measuring the hours, days, weeks that passed with no news of her husband. Little hope remained that the men were still alive. My mother, however, remained hopeful.

The others called her Little Audrey. When she arrived in Bolivia she weighed 90 pounds and looked more like a schoolgirl than a bride. She and my father had married on October 8, 1942. Mom was twenty-one. They planned to leave for the mission field a month later. Neither doubted their calling. Training and preparations took the place of a honeymoon. There was no privacy, no time for being alone. Audrey Burgess Bacon and her new husband soon joined eight adults and six children for a journey that began on a freighter bound for South America. Some of the children bunked with the newlyweds.

New Tribes Mission (NTM) began in the summer of 1942. My parents' group was the first sent to seek out a tribe that had no written language, no means of hearing the Gospel. The plan was to make contact, befriend the natives, learn the language, write the language, and translate the Bible. During the process the missionaries would help the tribe in every way possible, teach them, care for them, and tell them about Jesus. This was not a short-term project, but a lifetime commitment. My mother and father went to the jungle believing they would be there together for a long, long time.

After the men disappeared, the director of New Tribes Mission came to Bolivia and sent word to the wives in Santo Corazón that they should join him in the town of

Roboré, where others from the group were staying. The women could remain in town, at least until the baby was born. A German doctor there would attend the delivery. But my mother and her friend, Jean Dye, wanted to stay in Santo Corazón . Their husbands might return, and they were prepared to deliver the baby—just the two of them. But the stateside director of NTM insisted they come back to town. So Mom and Jean left their remote location with one of those two men who'd stayed behind, who'd searched for the lost men.

"I was seven months along," my mother later wrote. "Jean didn't want me to walk, but to try riding on an ox. I tried for a while but it gave me a terrible backache and so I decided to walk. It was a walk of about 75 miles!"

Mom completed the trip, but her thoughts and prayers were in Santo Corazón , where her husband might be trying to get back to her. Where she knew God had sent her. With her belly growing she wondered what God had planned for her future. Would she and her child return to the jungle? Would she see her husband again? God had planted a vision in the hearts of the missionaries to reach the lost tribe, but the first contact had gone terribly wrong. Was all they had planned, all they had prayed for over before it began?

"In you, O Lord, I put my trust; let me never be put to shame" (Psalm 7:1). "

CHAPTER 2
WAITING IN ROBORÈ

Paul Fleming was the director of NTM who came to Bolivia insisting Jean and Mom to come back to town. They both knew they'd be treated kindly. They'd be more comfortable. Things would be better in Roboré, but no one could deny the ache of two women whose husbands were missing. One day Jean came near the house with a letter in her hand, tears in her eyes. One of the men who'd searched the jungle had written to Mom and to Jean. He believed the men were dead.

My mother felt nothing but peace. "Jean, I don't believe this and won't believe it until they give me more proof," Mom said. She needed to hear the truth from the Ayorés.

Paul Fleming was there to meet them, and Mom called it a blessing to have him there with the group. He was a loving and understanding man. But even though the women were welcomed by the missionaries in Roboré, Mom and Jean longed to go back to the village near the jungle. The little house in Santo Corazón had become their home.

They never returned. "We felt so bad about it," Mom said. "But it wasn't what the Lord had for us."

Roboré, though much larger than Santo Corazón, lacked the conveniences of the modern world. Maternity clothes didn't hang in store windows. Of course, Mom grew as I grew. She made her own dresses with a big panel in the front. Cloth diapers couldn't be purchased, so Mom sewed flannel diapers as she prepared for my birth. I'm sure there were days when she wondered how she'd gotten there, how she'd ended up pregnant and alone in a strange country. To hear her tell, she simply trusted the Lord. This young girl from Michigan married the man she loved, joined him to reach the world with the Gospel, and put her trust completely in God.

"I always wanted to be a missionary," she later wrote. "From the day I was saved as a young teenager, my heart was set on full-time service for the Lord." She didn't know that so soon after she set out to fulfill God's calling, she'd be left in the small company of strangers to bear a child. Nothing about the trip to Bolivia had been easy.

But God had prepared Mom for the life he'd led her to, and she trusted Him. Being alone, waiting for my birth, my mother had plenty of time for reflection. She lived in one side of a square building with an open courtyard in the middle. The house was rented by NTM and had mud walls, a brick floor, a wall with a curtain for a door between Mom and four men. But the lack of privacy was nothing new for my mother.

The oldest of seven children, she was groomed for the role as helper to her mother—my grandmother. My grandparents were hard-working people who did odd jobs to support their large family. Mom kept the younger children in line. Her first brother, Ardeene, came along when Mom was two. Even at that young age, Mom was expected to help. Grandma stayed in bed for 10 days—the custom at the time—and Mom took her water and various items in a little wagon.

By the time Mom became a teenager, she was helping with six younger siblings, and her job was continuous. Many days Grandma worked all day outside the home. From the time she was 11, Mom held a job outside the home as well and gave the money she earned to help the family.

Life for the family of nine, in a small house in Saginaw, Michigan, was simple and never easy. Bathing was done in a galvanized tub using the water which had been heated on the kitchen stove. This water was hauled by the children from a pump two blocks away. They used a wagon to pull a large copper pot full of water back home. A single wood-burning stove in the dining room heated the house, but not very well.

In this family, shoes were for school and church. Each child got only one pair for the year, and they didn't want to wear them out. Grandma was a self-taught Bible scholar, and they always went to church, Mom said. Sunday afternoons were spent at the Gospel Rescue Mission. Mom remembered it as being the place where she came to understand the Gospel clearly. She recalled hearing a lady evangelist speak, and her words compelled Mom to accept the Lord.

Though the years were filled with hardship, Mom's memories were of good times, love of family, and God's provision. This filled her with compassion for others, and she knew the Lord had a plan for her.

Mom began attending the Gospel Tabernacle when she was a teen at the prodding of a lady who knew of Mom's interest in missions. Mom felt her pastor at First Baptist was not supportive of the decisions she was making about her future. Cecil Dye, she was told, would be different.

The first time she attended a traveling evangelist spoke, and the service was not at all what Mom expected. Her conservative background did not appreciate the fervor of the man. "He had a cowboy hat on," Mom later wrote. "He had cowboy boots on. Worse than that, he came off the platform and put his big cowboy boot on the front seat. He did it very nicely, but I thought he was very rude." She didn't go back to that church for a while, but that's where the Lord wanted her. Eventually, she returned.

When I was grown, I thought of Mom's aversion for a cowboy preacher and wondered how she ended up loving a place filled with spear-wielding natives. God changes hearts—that was something my mother learned as she followed Him.

God led Mom back to the Gospel Tabernacle, to the leadership of Cecil Dye. There she thrived and grew as a Christian, and her calling to missions becoming clearer. She could have allowed tragedy to deter her plans. In 1940, Mom's brother Ardeene was killed by a drunk driver. Ardeene had just accepted the Lord that year and was killed a week before Christmas. Mom's life had revolved around caring for the family, and this was a hard loss. But she kept her eyes on the Lord. She saved her money and made plans to attend Moody Bible Institute after graduating from high school. She knew this was God's will.

Even the presence of a special young man she'd met at Gospel Tabernacle didn't sway her plan to go to Moody. Dave Bacon was a preacher boy, my mother said. He worked for a business run by Christians, he preached in a little church, and he wanted to be a missionary. He and Mom began dating before she went to Moody. Mom went away to school, but when she came home for Christmas, the two got engaged. They planned to be married in five years, each having things they wanted to accomplish. But their plans were not God's plans.

Cecil Dye, Paul Fleming, and some other men were busy putting together New Tribes Mission. After Mom's first full year at Moody, a group met at Wycliffe to prepare for missions work overseas. Both Mom and Dad were asked to go with the group to take training.

No one was too happy with Mom—not Grandma or the dean at Moody—but Mom knew better. "Dave and I get an opportunity to go to the field, and I'm not just going to sit here!" Mom said.

"What makes you think you can be a missionary with only one year of Bible School?" the dean asked her.

"The Lord will take care of that," Mom answered.

After the summer at Wycliffe, Mom returned to Saginaw. One night a man from the church told her he needed to take her to Cecil Dye's house. He wouldn't tell her why, and she wondered why the man said to her, "It's the last time I'll call you Audrey Burgess."

When she got to the Dye's house, Dave was there. Cecil asked my mother if she wanted to go to the mission field married or single.

"Married, of course."

"Well then, you'll have to get married tonight," he said, "because tomorrow we apply for our passports."

They already had a license. No one knew about the marriage—not even my grandmother. Mrs. Dye's ring was used, and the two were married on October 8, 1942.

"What am I going to do?" Mom asked. "My mother has a wedding dress and everything. She's going to have a fit."

Mrs. Dye said they could have a mock wedding later. Dad took his bride home and kissed her goodnight. Then he went home to his own house. When they went for their passports the next day, they signed *Mr. and Mrs. Dave Bacon.* None of the rest of the group knew they'd been secretly married.

Dad had to leave town after applying for his passport. A couple of days later Mom attended a meeting with a man she had dated—Eldon Hunter. He would later accompany my father into the jungle. He could tell something was up with Mom, and he pestered her until she told him about the impromptu wedding. With the secret out, she knew she'd better tell her mother.

Grandma was so mad—she'd spent a lot of money on things for the wedding. But eventually she got past it and gave the two her blessing. The *pretend* wedding never took place.

Mom continued to meet with the team of missionaries while Dad was out of town planning the first venture. One day while Mom was in Detroit, Cecil Dye called her and asked if she'd like to see Dave. Of course, she was thrilled. Dave was having a meeting at a church with Bob Williams—another of the founders of NTM. Cecil came and got Mom and took her there. My parents talked for hours. Mom admitted she'd let the secret out that they were married. Dad was quite relieved.

The three of them—Mom and Dad and Bob Williams—headed back to Saginaw together. Bob said something about stopping overnight, and Mom told him she couldn't do that. She hadn't packed for an overnight trip. So, Bob drove to a department store, gave my mother some money, and told her to get what she needed. She went in by herself and bought a nightgown, then went to the drugstore for deodorant and other essentials. Mom and Dad didn't know it at the time, but Bob had reserved a suite for them. Dad carried Mom over the threshold of the hotel room and they spent their first night together as husband and wife. Needless to say, Bob spent the night in the car.

When the pair showed up at Dad's parents' house, no one there knew they were married. My grandparents on my father's side were a bit shocked, but not upset. They accepted the news with gladness, and Mom and Dad stayed there about a month, until they left for the field.

If Mom thought she'd grown up in a crowded house, I'm sure moving in with the Bacon family gave the notion of a big family a whole new meaning. Dad had twenty brothers and sisters! Of course, they didn't all live in the house when Mom and Dad moved in. Only six younger siblings were still at home, but the lack of living space meant that my parents had to set up a makeshift bedroom under the open staircase. What a honeymoon.

The large family was born of two mothers. My dad's mother died when Dad was 13. She'd had eight children—Dad being the third baby born to Otto and Anna Bacon. When his first wife passed away, Grandpa Bacon married Irene, and the two had 13 children together.

The Bacon boys were sometimes full of mischief, but always remained true to their upbringing in a Christian home. I've heard my father was a happy young man, friendly with schoolmates. While attending junior high in

Saginaw, he befriended the two girls who had lockers on either side of his. One was Avis, the other Marie. One day after school, he said to his brother Otto that if he ever had a daughter he would name her Avis Marie. He kept that desire and shared it with Mom. While waiting alone in Roboré, Mom knew that if she had a baby girl, her name would be Avis Marie.

Tragedy struck the Bacon family several times while my father was still a boy. A daughter, only five years old, became ill and died. Fire took two children—a boy and girl. Faith carried the family through, and when my father was old enough to make his own decisions about what kind of man he would become, he chose a life of service to the Lord. He attended Gospel Tabernacle and felt the call to missions. There he met Audrey Burgess, and the two joined their lives in dedication to reaching the faraway ends of the earth with the Gospel.

But so quickly my mother found herself standing in the doorway of the house in Roboré. Utterly alone, yet ever confident that the Lord had not abandoned her.

> *"Who shall separate us from the love of Christ? Shall tribulation, or distress, or persecution, or famine, or nakedness, or peril, or sword? As it is written: "For Your sake we are killed all day long; We are accounted as sheep for the slaughter." Yet in all these things we are more than conquerors through Him who loved us. For I am persuaded that neither death nor life, nor angels nor principalities nor powers, nor things present nor things to come, nor height nor depth, nor any other created thing, shall be able to separate us from the love of God which is in Christ Jesus our Lord"* Romans 8:35-39.

"My Father, who has given them to Me, is greater than all; and no one is able to snatch them out of My Father's hand. I and My Father are one" John 10:29-30.

CHAPTER 3
NEVER ALONE

The men who'd gone into the jungle to reach the Ayorés were George Hosbach, Eldon Hunter, Bob Dye (who was Jean's husband), Cecil Dye (brother to Bob and one the founders of New Tribes Mission), and my father, David Bacon. My mother's lonely days were filled by the love and care of others who shared her loss. Jean was there, as well as Cecil's wife, Dorothy. The women rallied to make things easier for my mother. They would be with her when she went into labor. A doctor was on call, everything was ready, and mom wasn't afraid because when she was thirteen, she witnessed the birth of her sister, Carolyn.

"I was so glad that I watched," my mother later wrote. "Mom was so calm, quiet and serene delivering my baby sister. She made it look like there was nothing to it." My mom didn't know it at the time, but the Lord knew she would have that experience in mind as she prepared to give birth in Bolivia, and it gave her strength and peace.

From its very beginning the journey to the mission field required trusting in the Lord, not just for my mother, but for all the missionaries. They prepared as best they could, but no one really knew what to expect. Surprises were met with kind and willing hearts, and a lot of patience. My parents left their honeymoon abode under the staircase in November, 1942, and traveled to Chicago with a group of eight adults and six children. With paperwork in order and a few basic supplies packed, their trip started where New Tribes Mission had formed only a few months earlier. Cecil

Dye, Paul Fleming, and Bob Williams had met with some others in a little room above a church. This was the beginning. Now the first team was set to go.

Mom and Dad, Mr. and Mrs. Dye, Eldon Hunter, Clyde Collins, George Hosbach, Wally Wright, Bob Dye, and Joe Moreno were the adults. Joe's children were Tommy, age 13, Mary, age 9 and Rosie, age 7. Joe's wife had left him with the three children before he came to the Lord. The Dye's children were Betty, age 9, Kay, age 4, and Paul, age 2. Jean and Bob were not yet married. She joined the team in Bolivia later on.

The pastor of the little church in Chicago was Doc Latham. He gave the missionaries opportunity to share their testimonies in church meetings. An old bus belonging to the church would get them to the next stop on their journey—New Orleans. Along the way they sang songs and shared fellowship. The comfort of the trip south on the church bus was a great way to start off. The fledgling missionaries would soon find their journey not so easy.

They arrived in New Orleans without enough money to board the freighter bound for South America, but they trusted the Lord to provide. The ship was scheduled to depart, but it was delayed for four days. While the group waited, a church in Chicago was finishing a week of meetings. As they ended their service, the preacher's heart was burdened for the missionaries. While the ship remained behind schedule, God's timing was perfect. The needed money was raised and wired to New Orleans, enough fare for the whole group.

The money came in, the visas were in order and the team joined other missionaries—thirty-five in all—on the big ship. Since the world was at war, the freighter was camouflaged; the windows were blocked with curtains. There wasn't much freedom to enjoy the ocean, but all the teams on board met daily for worship and fellowship. My father led the singing while some of the other men from NTM played their instruments. Cecil Dye and some others shared from the Word. Mom said it was like a little bit of Heaven.

The responsibility for the children was shared by the group. My parents were put in charge of Mary. She stayed with them in the hotel, even slept alongside them in their bed. Mary, and now her sister Rosie, slept in my parents' cabin. After two weeks the ship docked in Arica, Chile. There the team stayed in a hotel on the beach. Mom remembered that she saw a starfish for the first time there, and the group enjoyed the brief stay before beginning the last leg of the journey to Bolivia, but not the final leg of the long journey.

The rough seas were not so heavenly. The ship ran into a storm in the Pacific and swayed to the point that the dishes would not stay on the table. My father was terribly sea-sick.

The train ride from Arica to La Paz, Bolivia was exciting as the missionaries surveyed the foreign land and the variety of plant life. They wondered at the sight of so many sizes and shapes of bananas, thinking the red ones must be rotten. They soon found the strange fruit was edible and tasty. There was much to learn.

A couple with a group called Friends Mission met the team in La Paz, welcomed all 16 of them into their home, and fed them wonderful meals. Only Joe Moreno spoke Spanish, and the kind couple helped a great deal with interpreting, with taking care of all the legal documentation for the group to enter the country.

From there the group traveled, again by train, from the high mountain region of La Paz, down to Cochabamba, except for Cecil, who remained in town to attend to the few remaining legal matters. "Down, down, down we went on that train," my mother said.

Another missionary met them and arranged for a truck to take them to Santa Cruz. They rode the train to the place where the truck would meet them. Their luggage was loaded onto the open bed of the big truck. Dorothy and her children rode in the cab, and everyone else piled on top of the luggage. As with other parts of the trip that must have been so challenging, my mother had a way of giving a good report. "The Lord always met us and we had such a wonderful time."

Her gracious report continued. "As we went winding down through the curvy Andes Mountains on the very gravely, bumpy, narrow roads, we could see rain falling all around us, but none fell on us." Mom praised God for keeping their supplies dry, even though it must have been an awful ride sitting on top of a pile of luggage while the truck veered and rocked through the Andes. They kept dry, but the weeklong trip was not without trouble. As they traveled alongside a deep drop-off, the truck began to sputter. They made it to the bottom of the mountain, where the driver fixed the truck with a rubber band. "The miracles added up as we drove along," Mom said.

Bathrooms, for Mom, were another story. Every time the truck stopped for gas, she and Dorothy had to go look for a tree or a bush. Food along the way was strange, and water was never offered by the locals. Just as well—it likely would have caused more problems with the bathroom issue.

One night required digging out sleeping bags from the back of the truck—there were no hotels in the area. The last night on the road to Santa Cruz found the team in a hotel with unwanted guests—bedbugs!

But the first time Mom admitted to complaining was when she spoke of the hotel in Santa Cruz. She and Dad once again shared their bed with the Moreno girls in a room filled with huge cockroaches. Mom had something to say about that. She also objected to the tripe they had to eat when she gagged on the stuff and couldn't force herself to swallow it. She got down to eighty-nine pounds on this part of the trip. The team waited in Santa Cruz for two weeks to find out the next step.

Cecil flew in and met the group here. Another truck was prepared to take the team to Roboré. This time it was Mom's turn to fly. She and the children, along with Cecil and Dorothy, took a plane, while the men brought the supplies on the truck. For a little while Mom and Dad were apart. They had no idea that the time was coming when they'd be permanently separated, but they were doing the Lord's work. They knew He was always with them.

"You will keep him in perfect peace,
Whose mind is stayed on You,
Because he trusts in You" Isaiah 26:3.

CHAPTER 4
RUGGED PASSAGE

My mother used a saying when talking about the mission field: "The Lord undertook." One such time was when she, the Dyes, and the children arrived at the airport in Roboré. Not a one of them spoke Spanish. Mom fretted over what would happen to them when they arrived in a strange place and couldn't communicate with anyone. Then the Lord undertook.

The airline had sent one of its own workers, a man who spoke English, to meet them. They were surprised and grateful to have the translator help them find a house to rent. He even loaned them some dishes and silverware and helped in every way he could to get them settled.

A railroad company from Brazil employed a group of men who were staying in town. They lived right next to the house rented for the missionaries, and they spoke English. The men had plenty of furniture so they loaned some to their new neighbors. Two twin beds with no mattresses were not comfortable but meant some of the missionaries wouldn't have to sleep on the brick floor. Mom had the luxury of sleeping in a hammock with one of the children.

Here, once again, there was no bathroom, however, Mr. Dye soon had an outhouse built in the backyard. They still didn't have any toilet paper. Mom later wrote, "Fortunately we had our catalogs with us. Sorry, Sears, JCPenney, Wards!"

While Mom learned to live with the meager accommodations, Dad braved the rainy season in yet another long haul in an old truck. Other missionaries in the area had told them to wait until the weather was better, but Mr. Dye told them he believed the Lord wanted them to go. The trip took longer than expected. The muddy roads caused the truck to turn over on its side more than once. Each time it had to be reloaded with the soaked supplies and luggage.

What a celebration when the men finally arrived in Roboré! Mom and Mrs. Dye quickly looked over their items to see what kind of condition they were in after the rough trip. Only a few things were broken, and the ladies set up housekeeping. The adobe stove at the rental house sat on a platform in the backyard. Mom and Mrs. Dye had to learn how to cook in the primitive way.

The men had brought *quinoa* with them. The seed-like substance—cereal, the locals called it—had gotten soaked with kerosene when the truck tipped over. But the group didn't have much to eat, so they did the best they could and ate the stuff. No one told them to soak the *quinoa* in water. Mom could hardly gag it down and she complained. Again. About her attitude, Mr. Dye told her, "Audrey, you can't do that. It's contagious and it will soon be going throughout the whole group." He was sweet about it, Mom said, but it made her cry. "Audrey, you know I love you, don't you?" he said. This made her cry all the more, but Mr. Dye's kindness was genuine, and Mom never complained again.

The house had two bedrooms. There was another little room at one end of an open porch, and that's where Mom and Dad slept. The backyard was filled with *yuca* plants.

They boiled it and fried it and enjoyed the never-ending supply.

The men hunted and the group ate snakes, possums, lizards—anything the men brought home. One time they came back with a turkey, which had been on a rooftop when they shot it, assuming it was wild. But they had shot a family pet. The owners were not happy, even after the men paid them for the bird. Years later Mom still smiled at the memory.

She dedicated her life to the people of Bolivia, settled in with their ways, and worked alongside her husband, at least when he was in Roboré. When he was away, planning the excursion, she held him in her prayers.

Before the men went into the jungle, Jean flew to Bolivia to join the group. Five months had passed since her fiancé, the Dye's brother, Bob, had left her in the States where she would finish Bible College. The wedding in Roboré was held in June. Mom was the maid of honor, and Clyde Collins the best man. But the wedding did not slow down the planning.

As my father and the others prepared to reach the Ayoré tribe, they made their own knapsacks. They also baked, with Jean's help, several batches of rolls. The locals told the group to take the rolls into the jungle because they wouldn't spoil. They were so hard that my father broke a tooth on one.

Many days were spent fasting and praying. During this time, Mr. Dye sensed a lack of unity. As the whole group met together, he said, "I want you to know if there are any of you who aren't in agreement with this, then I hope that you will just step out. Nobody will make fun of you, nobody will criticize you. We'll just know you don't feel this is the Lord's will for you to go to the Indians right now."

Clyde and Wally had been with the rest of the fellows. However they returned to the team of women and children when it looked like they were getting close to the Ayorés. They were to look for the team of five men, Cecil, Bob, Dave, Eldon and George, if they didn't come out in a month.

When the men were ready, they traveled to Santiago, to the South American Indian Mission. From there they traversed by truck to the Tucabaca River. From the river, they went on foot. They had an idea of where they might find the tribe, but tall, thick grass hid even the appearance of a path as the men chopped their way through. At some point prior to the NTM expedition, soldiers from a nearby compound had ambushed the Ayorés and shot at them, so the missionaries took care not to wear anything that could be conceived as military.

Forging a trail, the men found water, or when they didn't find it they sucked the liquid from a plant. They built fires to heat the food they'd brought along and slept in jungle hammocks that were roofed and screened. A fire was left burning at night to ward off animals and even Indians, though the whole purpose was to make contact. Perhaps they didn't want to risk a surprise encounter in the middle of the night. All this was preliminary, a step in achieving their goal, and they came out of and went back into the jungle a few times before that last trip.

Taking turns, the men returned to civilization for supplies. When it was my father's turn, he was sent to get funds from the bank that took care of the group's finances. He stopped in Roboré for Mom, and the two of them went to Corumbá, Brazil, where the bank was located. For the first time since coming to South America, my parents were able to spend some time alone. On that special trip, Mom learned she was pregnant. She and Dad celebrated the news together.

When all of the men were back in the jungle, Mom and Jean decided they wanted to be in Santo Corazón. That's where the men would come out after they'd made the first contact. The women wanted to stay there to wait for their husbands. Mom was four months along in her pregnancy and because of this Mr. Dye thought the move wasn't a good idea. He told Mom he would ask his wife, who was a nurse. Mrs. Dye, too, thought it was a bad idea. But Mom was determined.

"Well, Mr. Dye," she said, "I've thought it over and I've prayed about it." Mom shared a passage of scripture, Galatians 1:15-16:

> *"But when it pleased God, who separated me from my mother's womb, and called me by his grace, to reveal his Son in me, that I might preach him among the heathen; immediately I conferred not with flesh and blood…"*

Mom believed God wanted her and Jean to go. He would take care of her and her unborn baby. Mr. Dye gave his consent.

Arrangements were made for the women to go as far as Santiago, to wait at a school. Mom and Jean got their things together and rode in a truck for the first part of their trip. When they arrived in Santiago, Joe Moreno was supposed to take them to Santo Corazón. But Mr. Dye had a surprise.

As Mom and Jean sat eating in the school's dining room, in walked their husbands. After months of separation, the ladies were thrilled to hug their husbands. They didn't have a clue that the men had been allowed to come out of the jungle to accompany them to Santo Corazón.

More supplies were purchased—dried meat, cornmeal and rice. Everything was loaded onto the backs of four rented oxen. Vehicles couldn't travel beyond Santiago because of the steep incline into the mountains. The owners of the oxen led the animals to Santo Corazón. Mom, Dad, Jean and Bob walked on their own. They took one donkey and enough supplies to make the 75 mile trip. One day Bob and Jean would use the donkey, the next day Mom and Dad would take their turn. The first day they walked only three miles, but each day they increased the distance. Being pregnant, Mom had trouble keeping up.

Nights were spent under the stars in hammocks surrounded by mosquito nets. The grass was taller than Mom; the path was hidden in the dense brush. On the last day of the trip, the travelers walked 24 miles. Mom suffered with blistered feet and fatigue. That day, Mom and Dad never caught up with Bob and Jean. The people who'd gone ahead with the oxen told them to meet at the certain spot, but when Mom and Dad reached the meeting place there were no oxen, and no Bob and Jean. As night settled in, Mom and Dad wondered what they should do. Dad said, "You wait here and—"

"Uh-uh," Mom said, "I'm not staying out here in this jungle. I might be brave but I'm not *that* brave."

"If I could carry you I would, because I know you're feeling so awful, and your feet are hurting so terribly," my father said.

Mom got up and kept going. The supplies were ahead with Bob and Jean, including the flashlights. The sky grew darker as my parents walked on. Dad did have a box of matches, and Mom said that it was the Lord who prompted Dad to light a match once in a while. Following the prints left in the dirt by Bob's sneakers, they knew they were on the right path. At some point, Dad lit a match and saw a fork in the road. "We praised the Lord," Mom said. "We could have ended up way off in Timbuktu someplace. How the Lord protected us!"

Their fear grew with the darkness. Suddenly, they saw a flashlight shining on the path. Bob had turned back to look for them. They were thrilled to see a familiar face, and they followed Bob back to the place where Jean waited with the men and the oxen.

That was how Mom and Jean ended up in Santo Corazón. The people of the village had never seen a white person, and they crowded around to meet the strangers. Jean spoke the best Spanish and communicated with the locals, who were friendly and welcoming. The two couples rented an adobe house that had no furniture, no stove and, once again, no bathroom.

Mom and Jean, at least for the moment, relished the time spent with their husbands. The men scouted the village for supplies, furniture, whatever they could find to make life more comfortable for their wives. They had a hammock, a wire-spring bed—no mattress. A table and chairs were borrowed from a local resident. One day the men showed up with several bricks of brown sugar. Mom wondered what they would do with it, but she knew the husbands were just trying to leave their wives with whatever they could provide for them.

The ladies quickly learned to cook outdoors. Three stones were positioned to direct the fire's heat, then a pot was balanced on top of the stones. As my parents celebrated their first anniversary, Mom cooked some chicken for the event. The pot tipped over, but they washed off the grit and ate the chicken anyway. They pretended it was breaded with cornmeal. Food was too scarce to let the special dinner go to waste.

My father volunteered to go back to Roboré to get more supplies. He walked the 75 miles alone. While he was there, he offered to go even further away, once again back to Corumbá, Brazil to get some things for Dorothy Dye. He couldn't send word to Mom as she waited in Santo Corazón for his return. After a month, she wondered what had happened to him. Finally, a letter arrived along with the supplies.

Dad felt strongly that he should get back to the jungle, he explained in his letter. He apologized to Mom and wrote that he loved her. Included with the letter was a little pink dress for their baby. By the time Mom got the letter, my father had already returned to his mission.

When Bob heard that my father had returned to the jungle, he went back too. The two young women were left alone. They watched, waited, and prayed from their new home. Though the village proved friendly, the deep, hostile jungle hung like an impenetrable wall along the edge of Santo Corazón.

"Be anxious for nothing, but in everything by prayer and supplication, with thanksgiving, let your requests be made known to God; and the peace of God, which surpasses all understanding, will guard your hearts and minds through Christ Jesus" Philippians 4:6-8.

CHAPTER 5
UNAFRAID

While Mom and Jean anticipated the next time they'd see their husbands, the men prepared for the day they'd encounter the Ayoré Indians. Cecil felt they were getting close, and he told the men to leave some of their supplies behind so that travel into the deepest part of the green hell would be easier. They each carried only a cup of rice, a cup of sugar and a little dried beef and even left some of their hammocks behind and bunked together.

This was the time that two men who felt this wasn't God's plan for them were permitted to turn back. Clyde and Wally went no further. That's when Cecil told them, "If we don't come out in a month or two, come in and look for us." The two men returned to Roboré to wait with Joe, Dorothy, and the children.

Back in Santo Corazón, Mom and Jean lived day to day and became better acquainted with the locals. They must have ministered there as they acclimated to the customs of the area, but their hearts and minds were surely set on what might be happening in the jungle. Perhaps the men had achieved their goal. Maybe they'd found the Indians and had been accepted by them. The missionaries were laying the groundwork to share the gospel to the Ayoré people in their own language—a language that had yet to be written on paper. This would take many years. The men were only taking the very first step in a mission that would not be accomplished for a long, long time. How patient my mother and all of them must have been. How gladly they waited on the Lord.

The time passed and no word came from the men. Clyde and Wally formed a rescue party. Don Roberto, a Latvian woodsman who knew the territory well, and Mr. Haight, who ran the school in Santiago, joined the group. Going in to look for the missing men couldn't have been any different than going in to look for the Ayorés. Clyde and Wally ended up going into the deepest part of the jungle after all.

The men did come near the Indians and a conflict resulted. Shots were fired, arrows flew, and some of the natives were injured. The rescue team returned with only a few clues that the missing men had been in the area—the Bible pages, a piece of a boot, my father's watch. But no sign of death. No bodies.

Mom, Jean, and Dorothy were not happy about the fighting. They felt that if their husbands were still alive, the Ayorés would certainly kill them after what seemed to be an attack by white men. Now it would take some time to attempt contact again. The men who'd gone in to rescue my father and the others could only assume they were already dead. But the wives, especially my mother, were not at all ready to give up hope.

So nothing changed for them. They would wait, as they had been waiting. Jean would stay with Mom in the little village and Jean would deliver the baby. Mom wasn't afraid to give birth so near the jungle without even a doctor nearby. But even though they weren't afraid, the decision was made for the women to return to Roboré.

After the long journey back to Roboré, my mother now waited to give birth in a room walled off by a curtain. The wait for her husband's return had to be left to the Lord. The jungle that held her husband, by life or by death, was far away. Motherhood, bittersweet and full of anticipation, was so near.

Dorothy planned to be there for the baby's birth, along with Jean and the German doctor. The railroad company had a little railroad car that held four people, and Dorothy had saved her money to travel to Corumbá to get some dental work done. She hesitated in going with Mom's delivery date approaching, but the doctor assured her the baby wouldn't come before she got back, so she made the trip. Jean, who stayed in the house with Mom and the four men, was gone too. Mom wasn't worried—there was plenty of time for the other women to return. Or so she thought.

She wrote, "Well, well, little Miss Avis decided she wasn't going to wait. I woke up in the middle of the night with labor pains. I thought, 'Well, this is cute. What am I going to do?'" She went and woke up Joe Moreno. "Joe, Joe, I'm having labor pains," she whispered.

Joe got up and put some water on to boil, then went for the doctor. With three men asleep on the other side of the wall and the children all bedded down in another room, Mom got ready to deliver her baby. Joe sat outside the curtain door and interpreted for the doctor. Back and forth the instructions went from the doctor to Joe to Mom. Nothing was available for pain, but Mom said there was no pain, even when the doctor told Joe to tell Mom to stop pushing—the baby was breach. Of course, there were some labor pains, but Mom said the Lord undertook for her. The doctor was able to turn me around and I was born without any problems. As my father wished, Mom gave me the name Avis Marie.

In the morning word spread through the house that a baby had come in the night. The men had no idea—they'd slept through the whole thing. Kay, one of the Dye's children ran through town saying, "Señora Adriana had a baby!"

I came into the world in a rented house in Roboré, Bolivia, on March 9, 1944. That made me New Tribes Mission's first baby born in the field. In my family were many firsts for NTM. First contact. First birth. First martyrs? That wasn't a certainty. My mother didn't believe it.

She could've gone back to the States—perhaps some expected her to. The mission field was not the place for a young woman to raise a child alone. No one would have blamed her if she'd taken her newborn and gone home. But this was her home now. She would not leave Bolivia. She and I would wait, and serve, and trust the Lord in Roboré. This was our life.

> *"I beseech you therefore, brethren, by the mercies of God, that you present your bodies a living sacrifice, holy, acceptable to God, which is your reasonable service. And do not be conformed to this world, but be transformed by the renewing of your mind, that you may prove what is that good and acceptable and perfect will of God"* Romans 12:1-2.

CHAPTER 6
SOUTH AMERICAN BABY

My mother wrote that after I was born, life went on as normal. She integrated into the community of nationals—the local population. These were the Spanish-speaking Bolivians who lived a civilized, though somewhat primitive existence. As a missionary, Mom visited the people of Roboré and the neighboring farms. She acclimated to the language and culture and found ways of ministering to the people as she witnessed to them. Meetings for prayer and study were continually held with the other missionaries.

An old baby buggy served to transport me, but it wasn't much good once Mom headed for the sandy roads on the outskirts. She purchased a horse, and I rode along wherever she went. Mom called the horse a real provision from the Lord and claimed that I loved being carried along on its back.

Being the only baby, I got a lot of attention. Clyde—one of those men who'd searched in vain for my father—took me for rides on the horse. All the men cared for me, played games with me, sometimes tossing me gently from one to the other, as if I were a ball. Mom never wanted my feet to touch the ground—she feared the dirt was too contaminated. A picture was given to a local carpenter of a large bed/playpen combination, and he built one. That's where I stayed, when I wasn't being held, until I learned to walk. I never cried or fussed, so said my mother.

I'm sure there was some fussing and crying when I came down with pneumonia at three months old. A tent was erected over my pen and tin cans were used to make a pipe for steam. There I stayed for several weeks, even when I was fed and changed. Dorothy helped Mom care for me. They took turns staying up all night keeping watch. Perhaps it was during my illness, when no one dared remove me from the makeshift tent, that Mom stopped producing milk. Cow's milk couldn't be purchased in Roboré. But once again, Mom said, the Lord undertook. "Well, if the nationals can raise their kids on oatmeal water and rice water, I guess I can raise mine on it too," she said. Until I was old enough to eat solid food, that's what I got.

When I was still just a baby, Mom began showing me father's picture. Every day she held it in front of me and said, "This is your daddy." She wanted me to recognize him when he came out of the jungle. My first word was not mama, but dada.

I learned to sit up, stand, and walk in my own little house—my custom-built bed/playpen. Mom said that she let me out once I could walk, but she quickly taught me how to squat without sitting on the ground. Even with her precautions, I did contract dysentery. Mom blamed it on my thumb sucking.

To hear my mother tell it, I was a fearless baby who would pry open the beak of the turkey who lived in our yard to see what was in its mouth. I loved animals and people. The lady who owned our rental house would stop by to play with me. She'd hold me up and sway back and forth, dancing me around the room. "My baby, my baby," she would say. Mom told of the fun we had—she and I and all the people who were part of our lives.

My first friend close to my own age was Paul, the youngest of the Dye children. He was three years older than I. When I was big enough to leave my pen, Paul was my playmate. There wasn't much for toddlers to do, but we entertained ourselves. One day, so the story goes, the two of us found some dried squirrel skins that someone had left by the house. Paul tied those skins on our back, and we played in the yard, pretending we were squirrels. Paul's older sisters made a teeter totter out of an old barrel and a board. The men put up some swings. A wheel barrow brought lots of squeals and giggles as the older children pushed Paul and me around the yard.

Much to Mom's surprise, Bolivia was a cold, cold place in the winter. My grandmother, far away and unknown to me, sent me a snowsuit. A real provision, my mother said, since I'd been going around with hands and feet red from the bitterly cold climate.

As I grew, I played with the local children—the young nationals. The sand street in front of the house was where we met. We pretended to cook, using my collection of little pots and pans. I easily learned to speak Spanish, as well as English. Mom had to insist that I speak English. She knew of other missionary children who couldn't even talk to their grandparents back in the states because they only spoke Spanish. She didn't want that to happen to me. If I didn't speak English to Mom, she didn't answer me.

Before I turned three, Mom was asked to move to El Carmen with a single girl who had come to the field. So Mom and I, along with Suzanne Plett, took the train from Roboré. Since the ladies took many belongings with them, they rented a cart and an ox when they got off the train. They piled everything on the cart and headed for their new house—one built of bamboo poles. My playpen/crib had to be left behind, so Mom made me a bed out of a big onion box.

Once Mom and Suzanne got settled, they began going out and visiting the local people. Before long they'd established a core group of believers. The ladies taught them in their homes. At first, I was taken along to these meetings, but Mom decided I was a distraction—a novelty to those who had never seen a little white girl. Soon she got me into a habit of napping in my onion box bed while she went a block or so away to teach the locals about the Bible. Mom later wrote, "I was either naïve or trusting, but the Lord wonderfully protected her and gave me peace about leaving her." The little group of new believers began to grow.

Even as a small child, I was given plenty of freedom to roam El Carmen—the people were friendly enough and the area secure. A nice man had a little store and he gave his customers, as was the habit of the Bolivians, a tiny cup of very black coffee with lots of sugar every time they came into his store. To not take the token was an insult and so everyone accepted. I was even given this little gift of coffee when I visited the store. Mom said I loved it.

One day I came home from the store with some candy, and Mom asked me where I got it.

"I bought it," was my answer.

"What do you mean you bought it?"

"Well, Mama, I bought it."

"What did you buy it with?"

"With my money."

"Where did you get money?"

"I had some leaves and that was my money and I went to buy some candy. That nice man gave it to me."

Mom must have smiled. She knew I wasn't a shy child, and she was probably glad the people of the little town were so obliging to tend to a little white girl making herself at home in their community. But not everyone was to be trusted.

A lady who cooked for the Brazilian railroad workers lived across the street from us, and I was allowed to go to her house and play with the lady's little boy. One day I stayed gone too long and Mom came looking for me. "Where's Avis?" she asked at the door.

No one in the house knew where I was.

"What do you mean you don't know?" my mother asked.

"We don't know; we don't know where she is," was all they said.

But then a man added, "She was walking behind one of the men, going around the corner, the last time I saw her."

Mom hurried down the street. After turning onto another street, someone told Mom where to find the man I'd been seen with. Mom went to his house and knocked on the door. "You have my daughter in there," she said. "I want her and I want her right now!"

"I don't have your daughter," a voice answered.

Bamboo slats don't make good walls, and Mom peeked inside. She could see my red overalls and blue shirt. "I can see my daughter," Mom yelled. "If you don't get her out here, I'm going to bang this door down."

The man brought me out then. Mom drilled me, asking questions about what happened. She concluded the man hadn't harmed me. After that, she said, she never let me out of her sight. Confined to my own yard, I still played with the local children. They came to me—I wasn't allowed to go to their homes anymore.

Our home in El Carmen was temporary. Before long we were back in Roboré, along with Suzanne. There I contracted a bad case of whooping cough. Even after I was no longer contagious, I coughed badly. People stayed away from me, fearing they'd catch it, but I don't think I started an epidemic. I learned to play alone, but it was about this time I did make two new friends. Bob and Emily Bodin had come to Bolivia to help on the contact. They had three sons, Bobby, and twins, Don and Ron. The twins, being eight years older than I, used to fight over rocking me in the hammock when I was sick with whooping cough.

I was four and a half when my grandmother wrote to Mom and told her that the family had saved enough money to bring Mom and me home on furlough. Mom's reaction was that she couldn't go. She'd been waiting for years and she didn't dare leave Bolivia with her husband still missing. What if he came out and she was gone?

Some friends—Bill Pencille and his wife—that Mom knew from her time at Moody now worked for the South American Indian Mission Board. Bill would sometimes come from Santiago to Roboré to purchase supplies. Just after Mom had gotten the letter from her family, Bill came to town and Mom told him about it, that she didn't want to go because Dave might come out of the jungle while she was gone. But her friend had an answer. "I'll tell you what, Audrey, why don't you just leave me Dave's clothes and, if he should happen to come out while you're gone, we'll tell him what happened and we'll take care of him."

The decision to go was as simple as that. Soon I left the only existence I'd ever known—life in the primitive land of Bolivia. In 1948, Mom and I went home on furlough. Only a few years prior, Mom had left the familiar for a strange and uncertain world. Now, that world was all I knew. Going to a faraway place called Michigan was *my* first journey into the unknown.

> *"Cast your burden on the Lord, and He will sustain you; He will never permit the righteous to be moved"* (Psalm 55:22).

CHAPTER 7
BACK IN THE USA

Not long after Mom and I got settled in with my grandparents, word came that the group we'd left behind had made that elusive friendly contact with the Ayorés. Mom wanted to pack up and head back, but knowing that her family had sacrificed to pay our way home, she decided to stay. Her prayers and constant thoughts kept her tied to the distant land where progress finally seemed possible. For me, family life in the United States became my existence.

Christmas in the states was like nothing I had ever seen. My grandparents brought a big tree in the house and hung glass ornaments and tinsel on it. Presents were placed under the tree, and I soon realized some of them were for me. On Christmas morning, all eyes were on me as I opened a set of toy dishes, pots and pans, and a baby doll in a high chair. Then I tore open the box that held a pair of ice skates. I'd never seen anything like this, and the puzzled look on my face brought laughter. A beautiful red dress, trimmed in lace, with a big white collar was the last gift I opened. So lovely, so unlike anything I'd known in my young life, the dress was later worn to a studio where photos were taken.

The little girl in those pictures only resembled the tot who'd played in the dirt streets of Roboré. I settled into this safer, ordered way of living. But even in the civilized world, illness found me again.

Red measles was the culprit. Mom had already had it, so she cared for me with no fear of contracting the awful malady. Soon the local doctor said I had to be taken to the county hospital and put in isolation. In the middle of winter, my mother bundled me tight and took me from the house. A single crib in a lonely room was where I was left. Mom said I looked like a little animal in a cage. My visiting relatives could only stand outside the door and look in. When they left, I cried so loudly they could hear me all the way down the hall. Once the disease began to clear up, a ward with other children became my new residence. That made things easier, but I was glad to leave the hospital.

Mom and I stayed with her parents for about two years. During that time I went to kindergarten—the same one my mother had attended. I had the same teacher and played in the same little playhouse. I learned to read when Mom was asked by the new director of the school in Bolivia to collect books to ship for the missionary children. My grandfather, a janitor for the board of education, had connections to collect the books. Before they were sent, they were read to me. Soon I could read them myself.

Mom taught Sunday School for fifth and sixth graders and spoke at several churches about activities in the mission field. Then, as part of Vacation Bible School, she taught a group of girls who were not part of the church. She grew to love the girls and they loved her. For the closing program, my grandmother put together a melody of choruses and practiced with the girls. When the pastor asked Mom what she had planned for the program, she told him that her mother was going to play the piano while the girls sang.

My grandmother was a smoker, and because of this the pastor refused to let her play the piano in church. Mom reminded him that it wasn't a regular church event, but he wouldn't permit it. So Mom's sister led the group a cappella. After Bible School ended, the girls wanted Mom to teach them in a special Sunday School class. They weren't yet comfortable mixing with the kids who'd grown up in church. But the pastor wouldn't give Mom a room. The group never met again, and the girls didn't come back to church. Someone at the church told Mom, "We bring them in the door, and he throws them out the window." This was the same church that Cecil Dye had pastored. Through this heart-breaking experience, Mom learned that not everyone was mission minded.

Back to my grandmother, Eva, she was much younger than my grandfather, Claude. She had run away from home at sixteen to get married. With all those children and so little time or money for herself, the one thing she enjoyed was the piano. She purchased it with the insurance money when her son, Ardeene, was killed. She'd taught herself to play and had been the pianist at her church for a time. Then she was told it was no longer allowed because she smoked.

She was always stern, but being told she couldn't do what she loved—playing the piano in church—drove her to bitterness. She was generous in many ways, especially when Mom and I were in Bolivia, but she became difficult to live with. We had no place else to go so we endured the trying times in my grandparents' house. I was expected to play outside, weather permitting, and to come in at exactly the right time for supper. When I was not at the table on time, I was sent to my room and I missed the meal. At other times, food was brought to me in my room, where I remained for days, locked in for some offense. Mom tried to reason on my behalf, but Grandma was tough and we were living in her house. One of the younger siblings, Carolyn, was just ten years older than I, and we played together. She even permed my hair. My grandparents' "surprise child", she was a bit spoiled. She was the only child still living at home when Mom and I moved in, and my grandmother doted on her. This made it tough for Grandma to completely welcome me into the household.

I knew, in spite of the tension in the house, that I was loved. Grandma tried to teach me how to play the piano. I remember her buying me an ice cream cone and letting me eat it in the car, even though she was strict about eating in the car. I think she meant well, but she struggled with so many things. However, that's a whole different story.

While living in the states, Halloween was a time to witness to people. Candy was simply an added bonus. When people found out I spoke Spanish, they asked me to sing a song before they gave me a treat. So I sang "Jesus Loves Me" in Spanish, then in English. It got me a lot of sweets!

The summers included trips to Bud Lake, Michigan. Mom's family would gather there to enjoy each other. I was the youngest so I received the attention. Uncle Jerry let me ride on his back in the water as he crawled around on his knees. Uncle Jack was home from the military service and he was so proud of his belly muscles. I found it fascinating to jump on him.

While Mom was away at a conference in California, Grandma took me to a revival. I wanted to go forward during the invitation, but I was only five and my grandmother held me back. She whispered that I should wait until my mother came home. Knowing what I needed to do, I pulled away from her and ran down the aisle. She called after me, but I kept going. Eventually, she joined me. When Mom came home, I told her what Jesus had done for me. She wasn't upset at all. She was thrilled.

Despite the generosity and the blessing of a roof over our heads, Mom said we would never live with my grandmother again once we left. At last, we did leave. The long furlough came to an end and we returned to the place Mom loved—the untamed country of Bolivia. It would be many years before Mom and I returned to the United States, and we never again went to Grandma's house for more than a visit.

> *"For God so loved the world that He gave His only begotten Son, that whoever believes in Him should not perish but have everlasting life"* (John 3:16).

CHAPTER 8
THEY FINISH MY HAND

While Mom and I braved the tough love of family life in the states, the missionaries in Bolivia learned the ways of the Ayoré tribe. Their odd, sometimes revolting customs were observed by those desiring only to tell the Gospel story to the lost. Tribal ways sometimes faced rebuke from the missionaries. Of course, allowances were made for innocence and ignorance as the growing team representing NTM began to influence the men and women coming out of the jungle to befriend them.

My mother missed the elusive friendly contact, the early interactions, and the first welcome of Ayoré souls to salvation. As well, she missed the reports of five men who were slaughtered by some of the tribe who lived near the Sunsa Hills, where my father and the others had gone.

First, an Ayoré woman was brought to Jean. The woman had heard of five white men who were killed by a different clan of Ayorés. The men's bodies were thrown into the river. Jean didn't know if these five included her husband. The men who were killed could have been part of a posse—ranchers who went into the jungle to capture Indians to use as slaves. But it could have been that the missionaries had reached this part of the Ayoré tribe. The location suggested it might be true.

Still, to throw the bodies into the river didn't make sense. The natives didn't make a habit of touching the dead. They often buried their ill alive, at the ailing person's request. This was their custom. Disposing of bodies in the river was not. And the bodies would have been easily spotted by the search team—the water in the area was shallow.

As Jean acclimated to the tribe, and they to her, she became a source of comfort to the sick, and was often called on to dispense medicine. One day a young, shy man approached with one of the tribesmen now well known to the missionaries. He knew something, Jean was told, about the missing men. Jean stopped what she was doing and listened.

The man had not seen the missionaries. In fact, he would have been a child when they disappeared in the jungle. But he had heard about them. They had come to his village, he told Jean. "They finish my hand," he said. This was how the Ayorés noted the number five—it finished the hand.

Tense and frightened at first, the young man relaxed as Jean spoke with him. He had not witnessed the event, but had only heard about it. "Your countrymen are dead," he said. Jean remained as calm as the boy. She asked him if the men were thrown into the river. "No," he said. "I think they buried them." That was all he knew. But it didn't sound any more believable than the account of the woman who'd reported to Jean. Ayorés didn't touch dead bodies, so how could the men have been buried?

While Mom and I were still in the states, Jean contracted malaria and went home for a few months. Of course, she and Mom spent time together. Jean shared the news she'd heard from the two Ayorés. She had doubts about the conflicting stories. Mom refused to believe them at all.

Jean returned to the field some time before the end of Mom's furlough to continue her work, living as a neighbor and friend to the Ayoré people, sharing the truth of God's ways with them, telling them about Jesus. As soon as she arrived, one of the tribe who was now a believer came with a stranger who knew of the five men, who had actually seen them. It was true, he said, the number of men finished his hand. They came in the morning. An hour later, the warriors killed them. "I did not kill them!" he told Jean. "The chief was away. When he returned, he was angry with the young warriors, and he made them bury the men."

On Sunday, a growing number of Ayorés gathered to worship. That same tribesman who'd brought the eyewitness report led in prayer. "*Dupáde* (the Ayoré word for God)," he said. "Thank you that Wana (Jean) has come back to us. Thank you that she is not angry with us for having killed her husband." After this, acceptance settled the wonderment in the minds and hearts of the New Tribes missionaries. But Mom didn't hear of this final word from an actual witness. Not until she had her feet back in the land of the Ayoré.

> *"And we know that all things work together for good to those who love God, to those who are the called according to His purpose. For whom He foreknew, He also predestined to be conformed to the image of His Son, that He might be the firstborn among many brethren"* (Romans 8:28-29).

CHAPTER 9
THE DAY OF ACCEPTANCE

The NTM plane carried my mother and me back to the place of my birth. First we spent a week in Miami Beach with some other young women who were headed for the mission field. When our travel plans were set, we flew to South America. Mom later told me that I looked out the window during the flight asking, "Mama, is Daddy down there?"

"No, honey," she answered. "We're not in Bolivia yet." When the green lushness of the country was below us, in Mom's mind, her husband *was* down there. Somewhere.

We settled in Roboré and Mom continued her work as though she'd never left. One day, Mel Wyma, who served on the ever-expanding NTM team, overheard Mom talking about my father. Mom's hopeful outlook surprised Mr. Wyma. He quickly found his wife, Connie. "I don't think Audrey knows that the fellas were killed," he said. "I overheard her talking and it sounds like she doesn't know."

Details of the deaths of my father and the others had been confirmed by the Ayorés. But my mother, a continent away, hadn't heard the latest report. Connie Wyma went to Mom. "Audrey, somehow you've missed the latest information about what happened to David and the others. Some of the warriors—the ones who threw the spears—have come forward. There's no question now. The men were killed." Mom didn't cry. She wasn't angry. Her husband's desire had been to make the first contact. If he'd missed it, no matter the outcome, he'd have missed out on his calling. He'd prayed that he would reach the Ayoré tribe, whether by life or by death, whichever brought glory to God. That's what all five men wanted. That's what Mom wanted.

Now, she had to tell me that my father was dead. She'd instilled her hope in me, and I'd grown to love the daddy I never met. I'd waited for him. My mother's peace in the matter helped me, and I met the news with a confident response. "Oh, Mama," I said, "now Daddy is in Heaven with Jesus and we're going to see him someday."

Putting the uncertain past to rest, Mom set her heart and mind to continuing the Lord's work. Life in the mission field had changed in the time we'd been gone and the changes continued. The uncertain future—no match for my mother's faith—was met with joyful anticipation.

The women who'd flown from Miami Beach were split into pairs. They prepared to serve in a number of villages where they'd gather information about the native tribes. Eleanor LaHue partnered with my mother. Mom's only anxiety about the mission before her was that I would not be a part of it. A boarding school had been established in Cochabamba for the children of the NTM missionaries. All of the other children went so Mom sent me, too.

Left with strangers in Roboré, I waited to board the mission plane with more strangers. Then I arrived at the school where I didn't know anybody. This place had a very long daunting driveway lined with trees. At the end of the driveway was a large white house. It was so spooky to me. It made me think of where the orphans were kept in story books. Sadness and tears filled my days. I thought I'd been utterly abandoned.

A woman who worked at the school had an apartment, and her little girl stayed with her, rather than in the dorm. Seeing my struggle, the woman allowed me to sleep with her daughter. Her kindness was appreciated, but it didn't make things any easier. Soon a letter went out to Mom, requesting that she come right away. Bad dreams followed my uncontrollable tears every night.

Mom came and spent some time with me. "I have to go and share the Gospel with the tribal people, and you have to stay here for now," she said. "We can write to each other. In just a few months, you'll get a break from school and I'll come for you." Mom prayed, and I knew she loved me. I learned to appreciate what she'd done and what she was doing for the lost tribes. After that, life at school got easier.

Soon the young women were flown to their assigned villages in an area called the Beni; Mom and Eleanor were the last to go. Mel flew them in his own small plane toward Santa Rosa. With only rivers and other landmarks to guide him, he got lost. Soon the plane was low on gas. Mel told his passengers, "Look down, and when you see a dry area, we'll land there." What none of them knew was that the Beni often flooded.

When they thought they'd found a good spot, Mel landed the plane. Dense, tall grass growing through the muddy expanse only gave the appearance of dry land. The water wouldn't have been so bad, but the plane hit an enormous, well-hidden termite hill, and the plane flipped upside down.

Mom regained consciousness to the sounds of groaning. Mel seemed to be in shock, and Eleanor was in the rear of the plane, trapped under the luggage. Mom roused Mel, and the two of them got Eleanor out of the plane.

Several families of farmhands lived in the area and soon they came near, curious about the contraption that fell from the sky. They'd never seen a plane. They mistook the headlights for eyes and became frightened, but they continued to move in closer. Mel managed to ask if anyone had a radio. They'd never heard of such a thing.

The missionaries were treated kindly and allowed to stay in one of the group's bamboo huts. For two days, Mel simply sat on a tree stump, showing little understanding of what was going on around him. He finally recovered from his dazed condition and permitted the generous people to give him food. Of course, there were no bathrooms, but they had corn cobs for toilet paper.

When Mel was able, the locals loaned him an oxcart to get the team through the jungle. One of the farmhands went along to guide them. Round eyes looked up from the swampy water—alligators filled the place. Not wanting to tip the cart and end up swimming with the gators, Mom and Eleanor sat very still. Even after all they'd been through, they rejoiced along the way, singing, travelling by night to avoid the intense heat. Eight days later they arrived in the little town of Santa Rosa.

Of course, concern mounted when Mel didn't return with the plane. Other pilots flew over the region, but the missing missionaries weren't spotted. Eleanor's mother, who worked at the boarding school, didn't tell me that Mom was missing. She simply held me and prayed. My mother, she thought, was gone. Just like my father. She thought I was an orphan.

The people of the town had gotten word about the lost plane. As the trio approached, the townsfolk came running and crying out, "They are here!" A radio transmitted the news that all was well with the missionaries, and they were taken in like family. Thanks to the local ranchers, steak and eggs were served at meals, along with the typical rice and *yuca.* Mel left the ladies in Santa Rosa, returning later with his brother to find the plane, repair it, and fly it out of the savannah.

Mom and Eleanor settled in a stucco hut and began the task of reaching the indigenous population in the area. Two years passed with no sign of the Ayorés, or any other tribe. But several locals were led to the Lord, and Mom knew her time there was not wasted. As for me, I spent school breaks with my mother, learning all about her work, about the natives, and about Bolivia. If not for school, I would've thought I *was* Bolivian. The language and lifestyle were natural to me.

Mel's brother, Dick, and his wife, Lucille, required help with the Ese Ejjas tribe, so Mom and Eleanor left Santa Rosa. They settled in another region, befriended the natives, and began learning their language. Mom reported that the Indians were cooperative, but mischievous. One time she noticed some of the chickens were missing. She searched, found no sign of them, and then asked the tribesmen what they knew. Their response reminded Mom of Adam and Eve. One would say, "I didn't do it!" Then, pointing a finger, "He made me do it!" No one would admit to the theft. The missionaries soon found this was the way of the tribe—the Ese Ejjas stole things. Then they blamed someone else.

While Mom worked in the field, I learned to live without her in the school that seemed so far away. Each dorm unit became its own little substitute family. I got used to dorm parents, who came either as couples or as single missionaries, only to find them soon replaced by someone new. Studies and chores kept us busy from dawn until evening. We wouldn't miss our parents so badly, the staff supposed, if we didn't have time to think about them. I missed my mother in spite of the discipline.

My early years in Bolivia had shaped me. The time spent under the stern rule of Grandma reshaped me. Life at school brought more transformation. Once again I was molded by my surroundings, prepared for the future God had planned for me. Preparation, to a little girl, sometimes came in daunting ways.

"Lead me in your truth and teach me, for you are the God of my salvation; on You I wait all the day" (Psalm 25:5).

My Folks

The Gang

The Guys Leaving

My Mom and Me

CHAPTER 10
THE AIM TO PLEASE

Dressed, hair combed, nails clean, beds made, room in perfect order. That was how each day of my life at boarding school began. Sheets had to be tucked in so tightly that a coin bounced off the bed. Clothes were folded neatly and stacked in dresser drawers. The inspector would check the stack all the way to the bottom of the drawer. A surprise visit to survey the room could come when least expected. Any violation resulted in demerits.

Each demerit added to a student's work detail or brought some other form of correction. Failure to work off a demerit in a timely manner resulted in more demerits. A chart revealed the names of all offending students and the status of their penalties. I tried hard to keep my name from being added to that signpost of poor behavior. Others, it seemed, worked hard at getting themselves added to the ranks of the tardy, sloppy and unrespectable.

After the early morning inspection, we were allowed twenty minutes for breakfast. The first meal of the day brought constant reminders to chew each bite 100 times. Next came devotions. After that, we had a full day of classes. I found early on that I liked learning, so the long days were not so bad.

The youngest children napped in the middle of the day and had fewer chores than the older ones. Evenings were spent in the dining hall. Of course, this time was primarily for studying and completing homework. Quiet students worked with no music or other distractions. We didn't even know what a TV was. We enjoyed the time, though, with all the age groups being together. This was where I grew up. I lived with many, had little time for myself, and missed my mother. School breaks were spent with her, but it seemed they never lasted long enough.

Dorm life had its advantages. I had good friends and teachers. I was safe and secure, away from the trials of the wilderness that the missionaries faced every day. But it seemed I could never escape the watching eyes. I couldn't get away with anything; not that I tried to here because I didn't like getting into trouble. My biggest fault was that I couldn't contain my laughter when others misbehaved. Perhaps I didn't cause any trouble because I was afraid of being caught, of the demerits and of the punishment. But I also wanted to please my daddy, who was in Heaven. He'd given his life to reach the unreached; I didn't want to bring shame to his memory. And my mom was my hero; I didn't want to hurt her. So I was a good girl.

The determination to be good, I think, led to some misunderstanding of what it meant to be a Christian. During those rare moments that I found some privacy, I read my Bible and prayed, or simply used the time for thinking. My deep desire was to love the Lord with all my heart and to do what was right. But I always fell short, or so it seemed. Every night I would beg God for His forgiveness, believing that if I died with any sin unconfessed, God would report it from the rooftops in Heaven. Everyone would know how I had failed God in my short time on Earth.

My child's mind didn't understand grace. Many years passed before I grasped the truth that I didn't need to try so hard. I just needed to rest in the fact that my righteousness depended solely on the sacrifice of Jesus on the cross. My righteousness was His righteousness and His alone.

Growing up in this environment provided me with a good education and a firm foundation in my walk as a Christian. But some practices of the school only added to my apprehension. When observing the Lord's Supper, for example, we were instructed to "make things right" with everyone. Students and teachers would stir, moving about the room, making sure they held no grudges and that no one held anything against them. There could be no sins between us as we took part in the taking of the bread and wine. How could I make myself worthy? My soul remained in bondage to my fear of being punished for my sins.

Bonfires at school were a fun break from the routine complete with marshmallows and camp songs. However, after devotions and prayer, everyone picked up a stick. We were encouraged to throw our sticks into the fire as a symbol of some sin we had committed. In burning the stick we were stating that we had repented of that sin and would not do it again. Of course, the teachers and leaders meant well. They only wanted us to live for the Lord. But what I interpreted was that I had to please God. Or else.

Spiritual emphasis weekends were just an intensified version of daily life at school. We lived with and followed the leadership of those who had given their lives to care for the children of missionaries so that we would grow up to be missionaries. Many of us did follow in our parents' footsteps, though not necessarily in their faith. Well-meaning staff members taught us things that either frightened us into following God, or else walking away from faith.

God is faithful though, and my childish, misguided faith grew. My understanding of the love of God, the simplicity of the Gospel and the freedom of following Christ came when He showed me that it all depends on His perfect and finished work. My worthless effort to achieve perfection in His sight was a fight that had already been won. Oh, the wonder of God's grace!

> *"For God has not given us a spirit of fear, but of power and of love and of a sound mind"* (2 Timothy 1:7).

CHAPTER 11
A PLACE TO REST

While I was away at school, Mom worked hard in the mission field. When I had a break from school, Mom flew to Cochabamba to get me. Together we took a cargo plane back to the Beni. Commonly, tons of raw meat were transported on this plane. Carcasses faced us as we made the trip with no seat belts, no cool air. Motion sickness was an understatement, and I always feared I'd vomit. We flew at 22,000 feet to avoid the Andes Mountains, sometimes dropping lower to go through passes. It seemed the wings of the plane would touch the mountain peaks.

A trip down the river in a canoe followed the last flight. All of this was repeated in reverse when my three-month school vacation ended. Of the three months, I had all of six weeks that I actually spent at home. The rest of it was travel time.

Mom had to keep close watch on me to assure I wasn't snatched up by the Ese Ejjas and married off to one of their tribesmen. One old man in the tribe had a 10-year-old wife, so Mom's fear was warranted. The Ese Éjjas were not permitted to live without a mate, and marriage came early for all of them. They didn't understand how Mom and Eleanor could be allowed to remain single. This was not normal or acceptable to their culture.

The tribe learned the ways of the missionaries and relationships with them became easier, but there was little in the way of seeing the Indians come to Christ. Years passed before other missionaries saw the fruit of my mother's labor.

She moved, along with Eleanor, several times during her years ministering to the Ese Ejjas. Dick Wyma's family lived on a large houseboat and they went up and down the river, visiting with groups of the tribe. Mom and Eleanor joined them on one such trip to travel to a village where the two ladies would live in a house built on stilts. Underneath the house lived a drove of pigs. Mom tried everything to evict the pigs, but they never left.

When the time came to move again, Dick came in the boat. Not realizing the river was prone to receding rapidly, he ended up on dry land. Though the ladies had everything packed to go, the river would not accommodate. Months passed before they were able to leave the house on stilts and the pigs that lived below.

After escaping the pigs, they made it back to Cochabamba in time for the annual field conference. This was a time of refreshment for the missionaries. They would come together from the various bases to share what was happening in each respective location as well as prayer requests and praises. A guest speaker would come to challenge and renew their spirits. A few weeks were spent in civilization. During that time, a visit to the doctor revealed that Eleanor had tuberculosis. Consequently, she would not be allowed to return to the Ese Éjja people.

Mom had a decision to make. She wanted to go back, even if it meant she would be alone. Much progress had been made in writing the native language and teaching the Ese Éjja to read. But others went instead of Mom, much to her disappointment. She remained in Cochabamba, working with Jean on the writing of lessons to be sent to the tribal villages.

Soon, others arrived to join NTM, and they were assigned to local work while they learned Spanish. A man named Rollie Hoogshagen came with this new group and served as an assistant to the bookkeeper, Larry Johnson, who was Jean's new husband. When Larry became ill, he and Jean made the decision to leave Bolivia. Rollie took over his duties. As well, he had the responsibility of buying supplies to go out to the missionaries who worked with the tribes.

Mom and Eleanor continued to room together in Cochabamba. The Ese Éjja primer and dictionary became Mom's work. Nearby, the new guy named Rollie lived with the single men.

While Mom adjusted to this new way of serving as a missionary, I made the move, along with my fellow students, to a new school at the foothills of the Andes Mountains. The leaders at NTM thought it best to take us away from the influence of the city. We needed more space, too. The new school was in Tambo, meaning "a place to rest." This was the spot where the natives stopped when walking from one city to the next. The new school was constructed just for us.

To get to the school, we travelled the new Pan American highway, referred to at the time as one of the most dangerous roads on the continent. Winding down into the lowlands, it had only one lane. Deep drops into the rainforest made us hold on tight. The older kids, and that included me though I wasn't very big, rode in an open cattle truck. The younger children were transported in a run-down old van.

Along the way, we had to stop and rest and use the facilities which, of course, meant stopping just anywhere and going in the woods. We stopped at a fountain that offered free, clean, ice cold water. Most of the local water was contaminated. We huddled in blankets, looking forward to seeing our new school.

I'd come to accept the other students as family. The older ones had played with me, sometimes pretending to be real families. One "couple" became my parents in this game and took care of me as though I really was their little girl. I had my first kiss at the old school in Cochabamba, or so I was told. The act of being dared to kiss the shy boy was forgotten, but the older kids remembered and told me about it years later. I did remember the good years at the school, and my family of fellow students. Moving to Tambo, all of us together, was a wonderful adventure.

The new school included six dormitories—three for the girls on one side of a square and three for the boys on the other side. Outhouses had three seats each. One of the after-school chores was to "keep the throne" presentable. We sometimes met up with huge spiders, scorpions, and snakes as we cleaned the smelly little buildings. One of the teachers allowed only one minute for a trip to the outhouse, which was nearly impossible, but I tried.

Tambo met hills to the north, a river to the east, that dreaded Pan American highway to the west and farm land to the south. Just across the highway, White Mountain was a favorite spot for the older kids to play a game called "Capture the Flag." We girls hoped the boys would try to find and take our flags. Better yet, they could catch us and take us to their camp. We often stole a moment to be alone with a boy as we played.

On hot days we found relief in the cold, shallow river. Girls and boys weren't allowed to swim together, so we had assigned days. At age fourteen, with Mom's permission, I was baptized in this river.

Though it was quite dangerous, we were permitted to walk along the narrow highway to neighboring towns. High school boys and girls were allowed to go on moonlight strolls, but only with a chaperone. We skated on a cement slab up the hillside to the north, played cowboys and Indians and, of course, studied hard and did our chores.

The move to Tambo added a six-hour bus ride to the travel itinerary when it came time to spend school breaks with Mom. Sometimes rockslides or mudslides made getting through nearly impossible. But I waited all year for the anticipated visit with my mother. I so loved getting to see her. When I was twelve, I learned of something exciting happening in Mom's life. At first, I found it a bit shocking. But soon I learned to adapt to yet another change. And I found the change both welcome and wonderful.

> *"Rejoice always, pray without ceasing, in everything give thanks; for this is the will of God in Christ Jesus for you"* (1 Thessalonians 5:16-18).

CHAPTER 12
SOMETHING NEW

Something old. Something new. Something borrowed. Something blue. Mom had always said, "I will never marry a stubborn Dutch man." In 1955 Rollie was the new man in town. He had been an army medic and now was starting his mission career. That new man, who had come in 1955 and was the bookkeeper, married my mother. At first, Mom assumed that Rollie was interested in Eleanor. Eleanor was certainly interested in Rollie. Since her friend wanted so badly to be married, Mom stepped back. After all, she'd been married, and she had me to think about. Rollie would come by the ladies' apartment and Eleanor would give him cookies. Mom simply stayed out of the way. But it wasn't the Lord's plan for any of them.

Soon Eleanor was sent to Tobité to work on language lessons for the Ayorés. It was there that she met the man who would later become her husband. Mom remained in Cochabamba, and her actions toward Rollie didn't change, at least for a while. But soon after Eleanor had gone, Mom was at the missions office working on the primer for the Ese Ejjas, and she and a missionary name Horace began talking about Rollie. Even though she was gone, Mom knew Eleanor must still be pining for Rollie.

"Well, Eleanor can have Rollie," Mom said.

"Rollie doesn't want Eleanor," Horace said.

"What do you mean he doesn't want her?" Mom asked.

"Like I said, he doesn't want her."

"Well, he can have her anyway!"

Horace left the office and went downstairs. Later, Mom went down and asked him, "If he doesn't want Eleanor, then who does he want?"

"You, crazy! When are you going to wake up?"

Mom later said, when remembering Eleanor, "I ran, she chased, and I won."

Mom had ignored Rollie, refused even his offers of friendship. But she soon changed her mind. Rollie wasn't sure what to make of it at first—this sudden attention from the woman who'd seemed uninterested. They began dating in July, and it didn't take long for Rollie to propose. Mom had always been concerned about getting married again, not knowing how a step-father would treat me. In short time, she knew Rollie would accept her daughter as his own. Their love for each other grew quickly and they set the date for September 16.

I was twelve and away at school. Mom didn't give me much time to adjust to the idea of having a new father. She simply wrote me a letter and told me it was going to happen. I really didn't know Rollie—I only knew that I didn't like his red hair and his big nose. I was allowed to go home for the wedding, and I had only one question: "Mommy, how can you marry him without me knowing that you even liked him?" But like always, Mom calmed my nerves and convinced me to accept Rollie.

The wedding was beautiful, and I really was happy for them until I found out they were going to La Paz. My anger resurfaced. I didn't understand how they could just go off on a vacation and not include me. That was how much I knew about honeymoons. I went back to school to finish the semester, and Rollie took my mother and my security away.

The newlyweds made a reservation at a hotel in Cochabamba for their wedding night. Typical of my mother's experiences, there was no room when they arrived. They had no privacy waiting in the lobby for quite a while as the staff readied a room. Then they were alone at last. Or so they thought. Someone kept coming in the room, then quickly disappearing into a doorway behind a corner. They'd been allowed to stay in a staff room, since no other room was available and the staff just kept coming and going.

The honeymoon in La Paz went much better, and then Mom and her new husband went back to work, spending the next five years in Cochabamba. Before she married Rollie, Mom had planned to go back to work with the Ese Éjja tribe. Since Rollie had an important job in the city, Mom's plans had to change. She helped Rollie with the purchasing, but soon she took over running the kitchen at NTM headquarters. The job was difficult but Mom, of course, handled it just fine.

I prepared to return to school in Tambo, but I didn't want to go. Even though I was older, I cried a lot, as I'd done when I first went away to school. I thought it unfair that I couldn't stay and be a part of this new family my mother had given me. But I had to go back. I struggled with that old familiar homesickness. The principal, Mr. Lotz, told me that whenever I felt like I wanted to go home I should just pack my suitcase and go. He was kind about it, and I nodded in agreement.

The next time the sadness and loneliness got to be too much for me, I packed my suitcase and walked to the bus stop. Waiting for the bus, I thought about what I was doing. Making a long, difficult trip alone? Disobeying my mother? Leaving behind my responsibilities at school? The whole idea of going home this way became too unsettling and I walked back to the school. Surely Mr. Lotz knew that, given the choice, I would make the right decision and stay in Tambo. That was where I belonged, at least for the time being.

A dentist and his wife, Paul and Beulah Mason, lived in the annex with Mom and Rollie. The Masons began travelling to the leper colony that was near Tambo, and they would come for me and take me home for weekends. That was such a blessing and made the separation from my new family bearable.

I did miss a good deal of school when I became ill. I suffered from terrible pains in my abdomen and chest. The doctors in Cochabamba didn't know what to make of it. Mom took me to La Paz, and the doctor found that I had an amoeba infestation. The illness lingered for months, but eventually I recovered and went back to school. I was approaching the end of my time in Tambo, and I actually missed it when I was away.

I returned for my junior year and found some distractions to my schoolwork. The first in line of these distractions was a boy named Dick. We'd grown up together, though his parents represented a different mission organization. Some missionary children outside the NTM family attended our school, as well as some of the kids of the American railway workers.

This blond boy sparked my interest during a period of doubt, of wondering whether God was for real. Why was it that the more I tried to please God, the more miserable I became? I didn't want to bring shame to my parents' mission work by asking such questions. Perhaps if I let go of the stern teaching then I wouldn't have to be perfect. If it hadn't been for Paul and Beulah Mason coming alongside me, I might not have made it through life at boarding school.

Since they lived not far from the school, they were always ready to come get me when I needed to get away. They even took me all the way to Cochabamba to visit Mom and Rollie. They were like a second set of parents, ready to encourage me and answer my questions. Even so, I fell for Dick, the handsome young rebel.

Like me, Dick was born in Bolivia and had dual citizenship. With his influence, I came to some conclusions about my future. Dick planned to renounce his American citizenship and stay in Bolivia for the rest of his life. Since I loved him, I planned to do the same. I didn't want to go home to the States if it meant the two of us would be separated. At seventeen, I was too young to make that important decision. By the time my birthday came around, I'd changed my mind about giving up my ties to America, and about Dick.

After that came a boy named Bob. I still hadn't come to the understanding that God loved me as I was, and Bob turned out be much too spiritual for me. I made a mistake with Bob. "You mean the world to me," I told him. "You should be saying that about God, not about me," he responded. That was the end of my latest distraction.

Last in this line of boyfriends was Ed. We seemed meant for each other. I'd matured and felt sure that I knew God's will for us. Being a year ahead of him at school, I knew we'd soon be separated. But I would wait for him, even if I was a world away in America. Someday we'd be married. That was my plan.

Talk began between Mom and Rollie about taking a furlough. It had been eleven years since Mom and I spent time at Grandma's house. Mom had been too involved with the Ese Éjja language material to think about leaving. Rollie wanted to complete five years of service before he took a break. When the time seemed right for the two of them, I was a senior in high school. Of course, after years of wanting to go home, I wanted to stay and finish school. So, Mom and Rollie waited another year. Though I looked forward to graduating, it scared me. What did God want me to do? I didn't know anything about the outside world, but I was headed for the United States. I knew that many of our missionaries came from the North Side Gospel Center in Chicago. I thought it must be a very large church. Was Chicago a state? I really wasn't sure. Was everyone there a Christian? I didn't have a clue.

Aside from marrying Ed, I decided becoming a missionary nurse would be my goal. Should I go to Bible School? The question loomed unanswered, but graduation day came anyway. Soon I'd be off to America.

Before we left Boliva, Mom and Rollie and I went to visit Howard and Maxine Morarie. They were the missionaries who worked with the Ayorés. So much had happened since my mother had first come to this strange land. In all her time there, though it was the plan at first, she had not spent time with the Ayorés. She hadn't met the men who killed my father. That was about to change.

A daylong bus ride through the Andes got us as far as Santa Cruz. We rented an ox cart to cross the river to catch the train to take us to the town of Porton. Animals were as numerous as people on the train. No one needed a reservation; seats were never guaranteed. Passengers lay in the aisles and we had to crawl over them. Of course, no bathrooms. Mom and I climbed off when the train made its frequent stops. We walked into the woods to find a good place to go, while Rollie stayed on the train and saved our seats. Then he'd go out to do the same. Stops weren't scheduled—they just happened. If merchants lined up along the track to sell their goods, the train would stop. If a traveler failed to get back on board when the conductor was ready to roll, he got left behind. We managed to all arrive safely together.

Howard and Maxine met us in Porton, and another rented ox cart took us to the Ayoré camp. The missionaries who had seen the harvest of the seeds planted by my parents were such a blessing. They took us out among the Indians and translated for us.

Mom shared with a group of ladies, with Maxine interpreting, about how her husband had given his life so that they might come to know the Lord. The Indian women were so friendly, so grateful, as they responded with hugs and tears. Both Mom and I were thrilled to meet the Ayorés at last. Even with the language barrier, the love was evident.

One of the warriors who'd killed the men who'd made that first contact came to Mom. "Señora, if I had known—if *we* had known—we'd have never killed those men." He apologized over and over. Some of the tribe, he explained, had been killed during the Chaco war. They saw all outsiders as enemies and they feared the men who'd come bearing gifts and Good News.

The Gospel did reach the Ayorés, and we were grateful. We offered forgiveness to our growing brothers in Christ. We were so glad to meet with the tribe and witness God at work in their midst. They have a thriving church, the New Testament in their language and are reaching out to others to share the Good News.

Not long after that, we left Bolivia. We were going home, my mother said. But it wasn't *my* home. I left excited, eager to greet a new world, not realizing how many strange sights and unexpected customs awaited me.

"…but grow in the grace and knowledge or our Lord an Savior Jesus Christ" (2 Peter 3:18).

CHAPTER 13

MY OLD FRIEND RON AND MY LAST DEAR JOHN

After enduring the strong odor of dead fish in Lima, Peru and the old world atmosphere of Honduras, getting off the plane in Miami brought a thrill, and some apprehension. We bought a station wagon and drove to Michigan. The sights and sounds overwhelmed me as I launched into the astounding American culture.

The year was 1961. As we traveled north, every restaurant and bathroom stop we made reminded me I'd been dropped into a different world. A world of black and white. Black people didn't eat in white establishments or use white restrooms. An entire race of Americans was treated with disrespect, by some at least, and I didn't understand. I'd never seen this type of behavior in my life. Such abundance, so blessed, yet America lacked gratitude and forbearance. My mother and step-dad had brought me to a new kind of mission field.

Mom had been feeling sick even before we left Bolivia, but she didn't complain much as we arrived at her parents' home in Michigan. After all, it'd been eleven years since we'd been there. Such excitement met our arrival. However, it didn't take long for me to recognize my grandmother's quarrelsome demeanor.

Everybody liked Rollie—he was a great friend to all. He'd become a wonderful father. But Grandma didn't like him, though no one was clear on why. I remembered her as being a giving woman, always caring of missionaries, so this was a surprise. Over the years she had saved dimes for me. One day I sat on the floor and rolled 400 dollars in dimes. Grandma kept bringing me more as I continued to roll. After a while, I asked, "Is that all?" I only asked because I wondered if I'd rolled all that she had saved, if I was done with the job.

"You ungrateful child," she exclaimed. "I had more at one time, but I gave some to other missionaries. *They* were grateful." I had nothing left to say.

Mom was feeling worse. She suspected she might be pregnant. She and Rollie wanted to drive to South Dakota to visit his parents before she got any sicker. As we left my grandparents, we promised to come back and stay a bit longer. But it didn't happen. Mom had an ectopic pregnancy and nearly bled to death. Her surgery and recovery kept us in South Dakota for weeks.

During this time, I got to know my new grandparents. Rollie's parents were of Dutch descent, kind and loving. They lived on a small farm with the youngest daughter, Joanne. The old house didn't have indoor plumbing, which was nothing new to me, but the little outhouse was the first I'd been in since leaving South America. Rollie and his mother and father would get up very early each morning because they had many chores to do and a big breakfast to prepare before the rest of us were awake. Every meal was huge. Farmers, I learned, were hard workers with hearty appetites.

Grandma had a large garden, and I loved helping with the picking and canning. Mom spent her days resting in a hammock under the trees as she podded peas and snapped beans. I learned to make soap from lye and lard. Rollie and

Grandpa stacked hay bales in the barn's attic. A summer of farm life was good for all of us.

Rollie even tried to teach me to hunt pheasant. I fired the gun one time. "I can't shoot this gun," I told him. "It kicks back too hard and my aim has much to be desired. " After that, my part in hunting was to run ahead and scare the pheasants out of the brush. Rollie did the shooting.

One of my favorite times of each day was to gather, with the family, around grandpa in the cool of the evening. He would sit in his rocker. Taking out his worn Bible he would begin to read to us. It was such a blessing.

As we prepared to leave South Dakota, Rollie was asked to help in the finance office at NTM headquarters in Woodworth, Wisconsin. My parents headed there to work. The promised trip back to Michigan had to be cancelled. Grandma got mad and stayed mad for years.

As for me, I went to the NTM Bible School in Milwaukee. The school was only thirty miles from Woodworth, so I visited Mom and Rollie frequently. Referred to simply by the address, I roomed at 618 N. 20th Bible school. Girls on one floor, boys on another. It didn't seem much different than boarding school, except we were all adults—close to it anyway. I was only seventeen. Some of the students were married and had rooms of their own. One of the single girls, Carol, took me under her wing. There were still so many things I'd not gotten used to. I'd lived most of my life with primitive plumbing. Carol was the one to remind me, "You have to flush the toilet each time you go." I'd never seen a vacuum cleaner. It was Carol who taught me how to use it.

This former hotel that housed us had a living area and kitchenette at the end of each hallway. We managed with only one bathroom on each floor. In the basement was a dining area big enough for all of us, so that's where we gathered for meals. Every student had chores, of course, and I managed to get some paying jobs as well.

Serving as a nanny was my first paid position. I made twenty-five to fifty cents an hour. Then I got a job at a screen printing business downtown, which not only paid better, but gave me the opportunity to ride the bus and get away from school for a while.

One night, after getting off the bus near the school, I heard a man's footsteps coming up behind me. I walked faster, then started running. But he came up closer behind me. I was almost to school when I realized he was a classmate. "Don't you ever do that to me again," I yelled.

"I was only trying to catch up to protect you," he said. But he never did it again.

My third job was serving in a banquet hall. We all wanted this job because we knew we'd get tips. Of course, paying jobs were not allowed to interfere with studies. We rode buses from our old hotel to classrooms several blocks away. Two of the students served as bus drivers. We attended church at the Wisconsin Tabernacle. Here I taught a Sunday School class for middle school girls. Years later, one of my students married a former NTM chairman. I rejoiced in this, and the couple remained a blessing in my life.

Before we came north, soon after we'd landed in Miami, my parents and I had made a quick stop at the NTM boot camp in Oviedo, Florida. There we met up with Don Bodin and his wife Jeanne. Don seemed to make a point of telling me that his twin brother Ron was still single. These were the brothers who, when I was very young, used to fight over who would swing me on the hammock.

So, what did I care if Ron was single? I had a boyfriend, and I'd wait for him to join me in the States. Ron was a "big brother" from boarding school, seven years older than I. I recalled that I wasn't fond of Ron's father, though he'd been an important member of the NTM team in Bolivia. He'd seemed a bit of a flirt. I surely didn't want to get involved with his son!

I did have fond memories of Ron. For Field Day at school in Tambo, I always wanted to be on his team. He treated the little kids with respect and he was so athletic. He could do more chin-ups than anyone else and he could go round and round on the horizontal bar. We'd played house together. He was always the dad, with one of the older girls being the mom. I was always the child. I figured I never grew up in his eyes.

We'd played Cowboys and Indians, sharing a horse between the two sides. I was always glad when Ron rescued me from the Indians. There were games with marbles, and we jumped rope. I loved double-dutch. It was most fun when the boys twisted the rope and the girls jumped.

Ron and Don both came to my rescue more than once. I had two little parakeets that stayed with Mom. One day, with permission, she sent them to me in their cage. They came on a truck from Cochabamba. Before I even knew they'd arrived, the principal told someone to let them out of the cage. Pets were not allowed, he said. I was devastated.

The little birds had clipped wings, so Ron and Don set out to find them. But it was no use—they were gone. I didn't understand how a trusted adult could be so heartless. But I knew I had good friends who cared about me.

When Ron began dating, I would chaperone. What could happen when two teens took a child along on their date? Wanting some attention, I'd stick a strip of tape to Ron's arm, then giggle as I yanked it off. No doubt the girls he'd tried to impress were not happy with me, but Ron didn't complain too much.

In the school cafeteria, Ron would use a small mirror to watch the girls coming in behind him. He studied them and they didn't even know. But I knew—and I wondered—like father, like son?

After that comment from Don that his brother was still single, I didn't give much thought to Ron Bodin. He was in the Navy, stationed someplace far away. I'd probably never see him again. I continued to write to Ed—the love of my life that I'd left in Bolivia.

The girls at the Bible school were warned to beware of the sailors who ventured into town from the nearby navy base looking for some fun. They were so handsome in the white uniforms, but we steered clear. When Ron's parents, who were then living in Chicago, came to Woodworth for a visit, Ron came with them. Mom called me to join them. I was sure that *this* sailor was someone I could trust, but I didn't want to go home that weekend. "I will miss my first invitation to help serve in the banquet hall," I said. Mom insisted and I went home.

Ron was visiting his parents while on furlough. He was stationed in San Diego and had to go back for his last tour of duty on the ship. The weekend at my folks' house was his last before he caught a plane to head back to California.

We had a wonderful time together sharing memories of boarding school and talking about our future plans. When it came time for Ron to go to the airport, I went along. It was there that something changed between me and my old friend. The tall handsome sailor dressed all in white was irresistible. He kissed me. And I returned the kiss. I'd made a promise to God that I wouldn't kiss a man until I knew he was the one I'd marry. Of course, that earlier kiss on a date in Tambo didn't count. But this one did. Standing in the airport I knew, right or wrong, I'd have to marry Ron.

Maybe it was just a friendly goodbye kiss. We *were* childhood friends. But it sure didn't feel like that kind of a kiss.

I went back to Bible school. Ron went out to sea. We wrote to each other daily. After his tour, he secured an assignment at the base in the town of Great Lakes. Soon we were dating, with a chaperone, of course. Since he could only come to town every other week, we were allowed a four-hour date, as opposed to the usual two-hour, once a week date.

Ron wasted no time in proposing. The bended-knee offer of a ring was forgone for a trip to the jewelry store. I picked out the ring set I wanted. We continued dating, but I kept Ed in my back pocket, so to speak, though the letter writing slowed in frequency and emotion.

The chili shop, movies, and drives to the beautiful lake shore park kept me enjoying the romance, but one day at the lake I felt we needed to talk. "I'm not really sure that God wants us to be married," I said. "I don't feel real peace and I have a check in my heart." The expression—a check in my heart—meant I wasn't sure it was God's will. I handed him the engagement ring.

He lifted his hand. "Then I'll just throw this in the lake," he said.

"Oh, no, don't do that!"

My objection led Ron to believe I didn't really mean what I'd said. I meant it—at least I thought I did at the time. I just didn't want him to throw away all that money he'd spent on the ring.

I'd talked to Ron about postponing boot camp. This was training similar to military training, regimented and intense. We lived in dorms and were introduced to living a deeper faith walk with God. Mornings were spent in Bible classes, chapel, and culture study. The afternoon work detail and games of volleyball were used to bring out attitudes. Each week we went out sharing our faith. For six weeks of the summer we lived in a remote area without electricity or running water. We had to make our homes out of tarps and lumber from the woods. This was to ready us for living in a third world country. I was only eighteen and I didn't want to end up going to the mission field young and single. I didn't like the way the young ladies were treated. A girl with no husband to take up for her had to comply with orders from leadership. After some of my experiences at boarding school, I just wasn't ready to believe that others would have my best interest at heart. I still hadn't learned that God was my Father and that he would take care of me.

I was only eighteen and didn't want to end up going to the mission field young and single. Even in my confusion, I felt God leading me to go on to boot camp right away. I wouldn't have to go out in the field until I was ready. I'd just take one thing at a time. At my graduation, I stood before the whole student body and faculty, my parents, and poor, unsuspecting Ron, and announced I'd soon be leaving for the boot camp in Oviedo.

Leaving Ron was hard and confusion followed me to Florida. But I knew there was something I needed to do. I wrote one more letter to Ed, the "Dear John" kind.

"You will keep him in perfect peace, whose mind is stayed on you because he trusts in You" (Isaiah 26:3).

CHAPTER 14
THE START OF A JOURNEY

The decision to go to boot camp meant I'd give up nursing school. And it meant I'd be far away from the man I'd determined I shouldn't marry. Missing Ron was no real surprise, and I tried to concentrate on other things. I planned to excel at boot camp, put my mind on spiritual matters, learn what God wanted for my life, and do it all with confidence. That was the plan, and I would stick to the plan.

But Ron didn't give up. He flew to Florida over his Easter break and we had a wonderful week together. With chaperones, of course, we visited Cypress Gardens and Bok Tower. Under some old oaks dripping with Spanish moss, he proposed. Again. His charm, and his love, won me over. I said yes.

Ron flew back to Great Lakes, and I finished my first semester of boot camp. The staff there turned out to be so loving and caring, and the experience was good for me. But I knew I'd have to do the whole training again once Ron and I were married, so I dropped out and went back to Wisconsin. I'd finally found a place where I was accepted, where I could learn about the Lord from people who didn't judge me. They accepted me for who I was. I left in May as the rest of the students prepared to go into jungle camp training. It was a sad day, but Ron was waiting for me and I longed to be near him.

We were married on August 17, 1963. The wedding was at the North Side Gospel Center in Chicago. We held the service in the evening so my Michigan family could be present. God supplied for the day in many ways. I'd seen a beautiful wedding dress in a store window.

"I don't think we can afford it," I told Ron.

"Let's just go in and ask what the price is," he said.

To my delight, the shopkeeper practically gave it to us. She even altered it for short little me. Even the cake came at a discount. Ron's dad drove us to several bakeries, and he never let me live it down that I tasted so many cakes. I kept coming back to Gladstone's bakery, my favorite, though I was sure a cake from there would cost too much. But we were able to get the cake I wanted, and we served it with punch, coffee, mixed nuts, and mints.

Rollie, the only father I'd ever known, gave me away. Art Rorheim, the founder of AWANA performed the ceremony. Doc Latham played the piano. He would have married us, but I had a notion that he might marry me off to Don, Ron's twin brother. He'd known the boys since they were kids and was never able to tell them apart. Not that Ron would have allowed it to happen. I owed so much to Doc. God had given me a good foundation through this man. So much of what I learned about the Christian walk came from him.

And he was a wonderful pianist. Our wedding song was "Because" written by Edward Teschemacher and music by Guy D'Hardelot. We were grateful to have these two godly men officiating and we were blessed by the lovely day that brought us together for life.

We honeymooned in a cabin in northern Wisconsin. But before we got there, we spent the night in Milwaukee. I thought a new husband was the one to make plans for the wedding night, but Ron didn't know about the supposed responsibility. We found a room—no bridal suite—but it didn't matter. We left in the morning, after a filling pancake breakfast, and headed for the cabin.

The nature lover in me was quite pleased with the delightful abode. We canoed in the river and watched for raccoons and bears at night. After a wonderful week, we drove through the upper peninsula of Michigan. We walked along the lake, went to a petting zoo, and visited Iron Mountain Mine and the Sioux Saint Marie locks between the U.S. and Canada. Everything went well until Ron developed an abscessed tooth. We headed home so he could receive medical attention.

In January, we began our training as a couple at the boot camp in Fredonia, Wisconsin. We both wanted children and saw no reason to wait, but miscarriage seemed inevitable each time I conceived. A minor operation took care of the problem. Soon after, Ron and I were asked to host the week-long, mission-wide annual conference being held at the AWANA camp just a mile away. We were so excited about this challenge. It was a big responsibility for a young couple.

As preparations for the conference began, I started feeling sick. I was pregnant and eager to see if I could carry this baby. A rash on my legs led to a trip to the doctor. I'd contracted German measles and strep throat. I lost the baby. We were devastated, but Ron had to go on with the conference. I stayed with my parents for a few weeks to recover before Ron and I headed to jungle training.

While at jungle camp, I got pregnant and this time I watched my growing stomach and knew the baby inside me would survive. We finished our training in December and stayed with my parents until we started language school in January of 1965. Eight months pregnant, I moved to Waukesha, Wisconsin. Ron and I lived on campus, studied hard, and awaited our baby.

Being a wife and mother was my most important goal. As a teen, I'd prayed, "Lord, please don't return until I have married and become a mother." Later in life, I realized the Lord's plans don't actually revolve around me—it's the other way around. But that was my expression of a young girl's dreams, and God fulfilled my desire.

She came a month early, this tiny, blue-eyed baby girl. Rhonna Marie, perfect and beautiful, was born on Valentine's Day. I fell in love with this five pound, two ounce baby. I gladly missed a semester of language school—Rhonna couldn't stay in the nursery until she weighed ten pounds. Our dorm was in a former hospital, our apartment the size of a standard hospital room. I stayed close to my baby since she had a problem with choking. With prayer and a lot of attention, she did well and thrived. Then I had another request for God; "Please, Lord, don't ever make me send her away to boarding school."

After language school, we moved in with my folks in Woodworth. Ron went to work to pay off our school bills. We had to be debt free to go out on the field as missionaries. The job as a line inspector for a tripod manufacturer took him to Chicago, and he often had to make the trek in horrible weather.

Three weeks early, on January 2, 1967, we got our second little blessing. We'd planned on naming her Ruth

Michelle. She was born with a birthmark on her forehead that stretched around one side of her head. When I saw her, I said, "God must have something very special for you, sweet little girl." I wanted her to have a special name. I'd seen the name Richelle in the paper that very day. It was unusual and I liked it, so that was the name we gave our baby. As a child, Lynn was the name I'd given my dolls. So that was the middle name I gave this little doll.

As Ron worked and we made preparation to leave for our mission work, Richelle was diagnosed with a hip condition that might keep her in a cast and keep us in the States for another year. We moved to Chicago, not only for the sake of Ron's job, but to be closer to our sending church—the church that would send us to Venezuela. Richelle was six months old. Rhonna was two.

I'd never lived in a big city. We had a small apartment that we shared with an endless supply of roaches. We soon found out that one gang lived on one side of our neighborhood and their rival gang lived on the other side. Our street was where these opposing forces met. The fear, if not the noise, made for more than a few sleepless nights.

When Ron was at work, I used a large baby buggy to get around. We kept it in the hallway downstairs. One morning when I went down with two babies and a load of dirty laundry, the buggy was gone. But God provided a replacement, and I continued trekking to the local coin laundry and the markets with my girls.

When Rhonna ended up with her head between two slats of the crib, her body dangling on the outside of the crib, I had to think fast. I put a little stool under her legs so she could stand, and then I dialed the operator for help. I expected a fireman, but a policeman came to the rescue. He used a handsaw to cut the slats, and Rhonna was released. But the officer didn't leave. "Thank you. You can go now," I said after a few minutes. He didn't leave until I handed him a five dollar bill. That old fear of authority washed over me.

Most days, Ron was gone all day and was impossible to reach. Once when the girls and I were sick, Richelle grew worse and I knew I had to get her to the doctor. I waited, praying for God to send Ron home. But Ron didn't come and I had to bundle up the girls for a cold winter ride—our first—on a city bus. I wrote down the address and showed it to the bus driver, who promised to get us to the right bus to take us to the doctor. After three transfers, we finally arrived. By God's grace we made it before the office closed, and Ron was there to take us home. That was the last time I used public transportation.

Life in the city for my little family would soon come to an end. The day grew closer that we would travel to a distant land, like my parents had done so many years before. The steel and concrete of Chicago would be traded for the lush and primitive land of Venezuela.

"But those who wait on the Lord
Shall renew their *strength;*
They shall mount up with wings like eagles,
They shall run and not be weary,
They shall walk and not faint" (Isaiah 40:31).

CHAPTER 15
FOUR TIMES BLESSED

In December of 1967, we flew to Puerto Ayacucho, Venezuela with our two little girls. We stayed in the city for several months, living in an NTM guest house near Don and Jeanne. Don worked as the supply buyer and bookkeeper for the Venezuela missionaries.

Since Ron and I had grown up in boarding school, we had the idea that we would make great dorm parents. We'd be more loving and understanding. Things would be better with us in charge. That was our plan, but God had other plans.

Since our report from language school indicated the two of us were suited to learning new languages, we were placed in a tribal situation. We'd written a paper on the Piaroa Indians while we were in boot camp, and that's where we ended up. As far as being placed in this kind of mission assignment, my desire as a single woman had been to go to the Philippines. I remembered how the women were treated in South America. But since I'd be going with a husband, the mission was met with joy and excitement. And Venezuela was, after all, a different country. Memories of the leadership in Bolivia were put away.

But Ron and I were still somewhat at odds with the system. When the rest of the team went home on furlough, we were glad to be left on our own. We were happy there and soon grew to love the people. Getting by with English and Spanish was easy. The kids had learned English from the missionary kids, and most of the parents spoke a little Spanish. At this time, there was not yet a course of study for learning the Piaroa language.

I spent time with the women of the tribe and visited the sick. Ron's days were filled with church activities. We never complained about not getting our dream job of being dorm parents. We knew we were where we belonged.

For most of the time we were in Venezuela we lived in a home on the bank of the Manapiare River. The missionaries who'd built the place went home on furlough, and we took up their work and lived in their house. Villagers came and went in the large house with a big open room in the center. The house was the first to come into view when entering San Juan, which was like heaven compared to other spots in Venezuela. With mild weather, fewer bugs, and friendly natives, we felt blessed to become servants there.

As soon as I knew we wouldn't become dorm parents, a new dream, new prayers began for my life in the field. I had four prayers, really. First, I wanted a home for my family. Second, I wanted a view of a mountain from my kitchen window. Third, I wanted a doctor nearby for my girls. And fourth—also for my girls—I wanted someone who could act as surrogate grandparents.

The last two prayers were answered quickly. The village had a doctor. And soon an unlikely pair took the role of grandparents for the girls. Raphael was the chief of the Piaroas. His wife was Eugenia. The two became like family to us, and they showered our daughters with love. My prayer was answered.

I drew a floor plan for a ranch style home, but it wasn't until the furloughed missionaries were ready to return that we finally got started on the project. Soon we were cutting the wood for poles. The wood was cut from logs at the right time of the moon. If not cut during a certain point in the cycle of the moon, it was thought, the timber would be filled with bugs. If cut at the right time, the bugs would not be a problem. We stuffed mud between the slats. We had three bedrooms—so much more room than my mother and I had in Bolivia. But plumbing hadn't progressed much—we had an outhouse. That didn't matter. God had blessed me with a home and my prayer was answered.

A screened porch across the front gave a place for the villagers to gather as we ministered to them. A mango tree grew in the front yard. Orchids hung in the branches, provided by the villagers who brought the colorful flowers from the jungle to sell. And God gave me a lovely view of the nearby mountains from my kitchen window—the last of my answered prayers. NTM planes had to clear this mountain range, and the low-hanging clouds, to get to the village.

The house was whitewashed with rubber tree sap to make it waterproof. "What do you think you're doing?" I asked the girls when I caught them scraping the sap from the walls.

"We're just making play food from the scrapings," they answered.

"You have ruined the waterproofing," I told them. "Now the walls will melt." It wasn't really that bad, but they didn't scrape the walls again.

We got some tin for the roof so we didn't have to sleep under thatch, and the bugs that thatch brings. To keep away the snakes we kept some cats outside, and we had the Piaroas skin the ground clean with a machete. Rain falling on the tin roof gave a soothing sound through our home. Rain barrels collected water. We had water from the town, but sometimes it would be turned off. Water in our barrels kept us from making so many trips to the river.

A cement slab provided a floor, and we even had an indoor shower. Electricity from town was about as reliable as the water, and it always went out at night to save fuel. But our stove ran on propane, our washer on gasoline, and our refrigerator on kerosene. We weren't dependent on electricity. Contact with the outside world came from daily radio communication to Puerto Ayacucho. And that was all. No TVs or telephones. Life was simple. The village had a doctor—my third prayer—and soon we built a chicken coop and bought some hens, so we had fresh eggs. Rhonna and Richelle used their little buckets to gather the eggs until the day they were met at the coop by a big green iguana. We heard iguana meat was good to eat, but we never tried it. We did, however, occasionally have to eat one of our chickens. The Piaroas thought we were terrible to eat our own pets. Sometimes that was all we had.

Other than this sort of occasional misunderstanding, the Piaroas were good people, kind and generous. We served in the little village and shared the Gospel with the people there for three and a half years. During our last few months in the field, we began a course of study for learning the Piaroa language. This was so important to translating the Bible into the native language, so we focused a great deal of our time on the task. Pleased with the progress, and happily serving in every way, we were surprised by a visit from two leaders who flew in to see us before we went home on furlough.

We were shocked to hear them say that we wouldn't be returning to Venezuela until we had repeated at least one semester of boot camp. A letter had been passed on from our first round of boot camp in Wisconsin. Some problems were mentioned in the letter and leadership believed those problems had not been resolved. We weren't doing our part, they said, and someone had a check in his heart about letting us go on.

In May of 1971, we went home downcast and didn't know if we'd ever try again. We'd lived in our home—my answered prayer—only eight months. Now it seemed we might never return. We didn't go to the first semester of boot camp available for us when we returned to the states, but waited until January of 1972. Our hearts and our attitudes were bitter. We felt we'd lost everything we'd worked for. Little did we know, but God, like always, had something better planned for us.

"Behold, children are a heritage from the Lord" (Psalm 127:3).

CHAPTER 16
GRATEFULLY LED

Boot camp was, once again, a time of joy and learning. The leadership and the students cared for us and accepted us for who we were. We had, for most of our lives, obeyed without question. We kept our opinions, our needs, our concerns, and our fears to ourselves. If we had a serious problem, we didn't speak of it, believing the response of others would be that we simply weren't trusting the Lord. Godly people didn't have problems. But we did. Boot camp turned out to be a place of healing, or facing our difficulties in an environment of love.

Our home at jungle camp was an example to others in training with us. We built it from logs and tarps. Our tabletop was made from dirt packed inside a tarp, our bed from logs and ropes. We even had running water—we ran to the well for it.

Rhonna and Richelle enjoyed being outdoors and living the way they did overseas. Our hearts softened, and we began to put our problems behind us. Then something happened that brought an end, once again, to our contentment.

Ron went in a canoe with some of the other men to pick up supplies in town. The canoe tipped and he fell onto the rocks, hitting hard with his knee. The doctor in town drained fluid from the injured knee, then advised Ron not to return to camp. The knee would take some time to heal.

"Why, Lord, do we keep getting bumped around? We were having so much fun at camp as a family. What are we going to do now?" This was our frustrated prayer. We didn't understand how God could allow this to happen. We hadn't even finished our semester. But God, of course, worked things out the way He wanted.

The maintenance man at NTM headquarters in Woodworth had left for another job. Winter was coming and the boiler needed to be hooked up to heat the building. Back in 1956, when Ron first came home from Bolivia, he'd worked on the plumbing in this same building, so Rollie called and told Ron about the need, then asked the leadership to allow us to move there for a few months to help out. So we packed up and moved to Woodworth. We settled into an apartment, glad to be spending some time near my parents. Our apartment next to the single women's dorm and the finance office was in a building where vaccines had been manufactured. It wasn't the best place to set up housekeeping, but several families called it home. The property was beautiful with large trees lining the driveway. The main home of the previous owner was at the front of the property, and it was made into three apartments for some of the leaders. My parents lived in a house that was once a stable on the property. The lovely little white home was a place of refuge for my sweet mom. After so many years in the field, and with her tumultuous relationship with my grandmother, she needed a quiet place of her own.

We quickly grew to love the place. I walked the rim of the property, enjoying God's beauty as the leaves changed in the fall. The walks were mini vacations for me, and the Lord always gave me His joy. The girls had lots of room to run and play.

Before long, that maintenance man returned needing his old job back. Once again, we were left wondering what our future held. And once again, Rollie called the leadership. He asked if Ron could help him in the finance office. The membership was growing and Rollie needed the help.

Many years earlier, in the 1950's in Bolivia, the two had roomed together in the men's dorm never dreaming they'd marry the Bacon girls—my mom and me.

Ron took the position, and this is where we stayed. We hadn't expected to stay in the U.S., and we certainly didn't expect to be blessed with the opportunity to live so close to my parents, but that's what God had planned. It was a true blessing and we thanked God.

A few years went by, and then two more blessings came along. I'd had an ectopic pregnancy in 1973 and didn't expect to have any more children. But in January of 1975, Ruthie JoyAnn was born, and then in December of 1976, we had our boy, Robert Ray Nathan. Our little apartment was too small for six, and so Rhonna and Richelle slept in a room in the girls' dorm. They were just eight and ten, and having a bedroom in the dorm was quite an adventure for them.

The New Tribes Mission organization, not to mention my own family, had outgrown our place in Woodworth. The search for new property began. There was talk of a building in Jackson, Mississippi. Our children's only outdoor play area would have been on a rooftop. Another property in Nebraska was considered. Neither of these options worked out. But soon the Lord gave us a large run-down hotel and surrounding property in Sanford, Florida. NTM took great pleasure in buying up old properties in need of much repair—the price was right—and turning them into facilities where our missionaries could live and work.

In 1977 a group moved to Sanford, took up residence in the little former motel beside the old grand hotel, circa 1925, and began the renovations. The naval academy had been the last to use the building and the place was a mess. Everything had to be brought up to code. Students went from our various training facilities to spend several weeks working. When they returned, another group would go. Long before the work was done, the finance office made their move south. They couldn't be down for long since the missionaries had to receive their vouchers on time. When the work was done at the end of the month, the very large and difficult to move IBM machines were loaded into trucks. Everything was set up and running at the new headquarters before the next vouchers were due to go out.

Ron and our two oldest girls made the trip in a truck with a trailer in tow. When they left, I took Ruthie and Rob to stay with the family that was going to take us to the airport the next day. We had no way of communicating, so I didn't know how Ron and the girls were doing as they drove through a blizzard, and they didn't know that I was snowbound. When the children and I finally were able to leave, the wind-chill was minus sixty degrees. When we landed in Florida, the temperature was ninety degrees.

Eighteen families moved from Woodworth. We were placed in housing by a real estate agent in Sanford until our new apartment homes were ready. Our temporary home was a small apartment that we shared with Mom and Rollie and my Aunt Beverly—Mom's sister—who came south with us to escape an abusive husband.

One of the first things to do was to find a school for Rhonna and Richelle. We chose a church school in Deltona, a community on the other side of Lake Monroe from our new headquarters. A rickety old van came to town to pick up the girls every morning and take them to the other side of the huge lake, which was part of the St. Johns River.

Ron had made a trip to the property before me. "Please take it all in slowly as you look at it," he told me. I didn't know what to expect. The enormous building had a tile Spanish roof. Apartments in the south side of the building would be much warmer than on the north—the lake side. Our apartment would be on the south side. The day I was able to get to the building brought only shock. It was so big, and so much work still had to be done. But the view of the lake with a large grassy area extending toward the waterfront was amazing.

Once again, my only transportation was my own two feet and a stroller. Every day I packed up supplies for Ruthie, age three, and pushed her in the stroller to spend the day working on our apartment at the headquarters. I'd find the cleanest place for her to play, and I put a mattress in what would become our laundry room for her take naps. Rob stayed with Mom and Auntie. I took him a few times, but when he climbed up on a windowsill in the second-floor apartment—it had no glass or screen—I refused to take him anymore.

I worked hard on the remodeling, burning or scraping paint off seventeen huge wooden doors and seven large double window frames. We had no running water in our end of the building and no light fixtures at first, so the work went slow. We shopped for used carpet for the seven rooms of our apartment, got our kitchen in working order, and then moved in. It wasn't quite finished, but we were glad to be in our own home. Mom and Rollie moved into their apartment and Aunt Beverly stayed with them until she got a job and a place to live. We set up the dining room and enjoyed meals together.

A kind of blessed chaos resulted when Ron's parents came to stay with us while they waited for their new home in south Florida to be ready. We'd helped them move from Pennsylvania. Here we were in hot and sunny Florida with four kids, two sets of grandparents, and an aunt. At the time, it was *not* fun. Fire code had put an end to the open breezeways of the old hotel. Of course, it wasn't air-conditioned. Eventually we got a window unit—what a blessing. After six months of working evenings and Saturdays, the large pool was ready—another blessing that gave relief from the heat. We knew this was a luxury, not a necessity, but we were all glad to spend our off hours repairing it.

And so life went on as we served in administration for our missionaries throughout the world, worked in the local church, and raised our family. Goodness followed us as we followed God's will. Of course, bad times came along. Some of them were very bad. The years ahead of us would challenge our faith and our sense of belonging. Seeking the will of God, we could only keep going when we were met with misunderstanding and judgment. What would it take for us to truly understand the awesome grace of God?

"Trust in the Lord with all your heart,
and lean not on your own understanding;
In all your ways acknowledge Him,
and He shall direct your paths" (Proverbs 3:5-6).

CHAPTER 17
FORGIVENESS

Our years at NTM headquarters in Sanford were a mix of working hard for the organization, raising kids, and serving in the local church. Our place of service was Central Baptist Church. We received so much there in the way of training and discipleship and gave of ourselves in ministries involving music and children. Conferences in Ridgecrest, North Carolina provided great times of refreshing and gaining resources.

Our service with NTM didn't always offer as great a reward as our church life. Ron's job brought stress, as all jobs do. I faced the challenge of being required to work as well, while trying to raise my children—two roles I never quite managed to effectively blend. I complained about the office work that NTM assigned to all the women, no matter their maternal calling. Ron, to some, came across as unapproachable and difficult as he worked in the finance department. We were both, it seemed, wrought with perpetual bad attitudes.

Despite the occasional rift, we thought we were doing okay. Rhonna and Richelle grew into adulthood, with Ruthie and Rob not too far behind. For some couples the challenges brought on by life only brings them closer. Ron and I found this wasn't always true for us. But our problems, like always, were pushed too far down to see. The result was discontent, quiet and hidden. Keeping it all presentable was what mattered. But God loved us and didn't leave us in the mess we'd made. Of course, God's discipline sometimes hurts.

In 1993, an edict came from a committee. A letter was composed to give us full understanding of the decision made by some of our friends and co-workers. Ron and I were no longer needed at New Tribes Mission. We were to pack our belongings and leave headquarters immediately. No other mission field had a place for us. We should get on with our lives. Elsewhere.

We were shocked, wounded beyond words, and left with an uncertain future. But we were not without a smidgen of support. Our principal from the boarding school—the one who'd set my little birds free and hurt me so badly—put a stop to the ousting. It wasn't the way to handle problems within the organization, he said. Others listened to reason and we were allowed to stay. But the damage was done.

In the year that followed, my health suffered. I lost all stamina, then developed Type 2 Diabetes. Still, we held on to our attitudes, perhaps an unhealthy dose of righteous indignation. And we were unforgiving. Five years passed before another burden finally completed the work God had started in us when he turned our lives upside down.

Cancer was the persuading factor. Ron was diagnosed in October of 1998. Six weeks of unrelenting chemo were followed by thirty radiation treatments. In January, parts of his stomach and esophagus were removed. He spent nine months on a feeding tube. He could do nothing. I could do nothing but care for him. When it was over, we didn't regret it at all.

During that time God challenged us to pray for our accusers—for the ones behind our problems with NTM.

As we prayed, forgiveness came. And understanding. Far from perfect in our service, harboring resentment in our hearts, we accepted that we needed God's grace as much as anyone. Maybe more. To God be the glory—the experience healed us. Our marriage became a blessing, and our work became an offering of honor to the One for whom we worked.

When we were a family of four, we moved to a smaller apartment across the street from the main building. All of us at NTM were surprised when a lovely neighborhood of retirement homes was built a couple of miles from headquarters. Mom and Rollie moved in 1999 to Panama Place. Just two days before Christmas 2001, Ron and I moved into our little duplex on Mexico Court. All the streets were named for countries that had been impacted by the work of the missionaries.

Moving, of course, didn't come without some hesitation and difficulties. Our move in 2001 came before our actual retirement. I wasn't so sure I was ready to live there—I thought I was too young. Finances would also be an issue as becoming a resident there didn't come without a cost. We hadn't done much planning for retirement, and we didn't have any savings to speak of. It was Rollie who'd invested and done well with some stock purchases. His generosity allowed us to make the move, but it was God's provision that put us in the right place.

Only a year later, Rollie went home to be with Jesus. He'd been a real father to me, and I'd accepted God's love as my heavenly Father. But I had a father I never knew, and I dreamed of returning to the place where he gave up his life.

"Let all bitterness, wrath, anger, clamor, and evil speaking be put away from you, with all malice. 32 And be kind to one another, tenderhearted, forgiving one another, even as God in Christ forgave you" (Ephesians 4:31-32).

CHAPTER 18
THE LONG ROAD BACK

Bolivia, the land of my birth, frequently called to me in my imagination. I wanted to go back, to retrace the steps of my parents. For years, Rollie said he would pay my way. "Just take your mother with you," he said. He had no desire to return, and Mom wouldn't go without him. After he passed, I thought I'd never be able to go.

Then in 2004, Richelle heard about a women's conference to be held in Bolivia. "Mom, do you want to go?" she asked.

"Of course I want to go!" I told her. But I wanted a couple of days to visit the place of my birth, maybe meet with the Ayorés. The men who'd killed my father and the others were probably all dead, but perhaps I could find some of their descendants. My excitement grew as I thought of the prospect. Some would question my reason for desiring such a meeting. I only wanted to see for myself that my father's death was not in vain. And I wanted to demonstrate forgiveness to these people. I held no ill against them.

The trip was organized by a lady from a church in Oviedo, who held retreats for women in fulltime ministry around the world. My plan to revisit the places of my childhood came together. The first week was set aside for leading Vacation Bible School, then heading to a retreat center. The second week would take me to the places my parents had been. I'd even go back to boarding school, but for a reason that would be bittersweet.

Cochabamba was where we traveled with the other ladies. The conference was a time of rest and refreshing for the ladies. I served on the team of hosts at the center that had been reserved for us at no cost to the guests. The week was wonderful, but when Saturday came my adventure really began.

Richelle and I got up at four in the morning to catch the flight from Cochabamba in the highlands to Santa Cruz in the lowland. A photographer named Donna joined us, and we were met by a missionary named Steve, who took us to where our pilot waited with his six-passenger Cessna that I'd reserved.

The pilot, Greg, was a single missionary who flew for South American Mission. He'd been flying for thirteen years, but only one of those years in Bolivia. NTM planes no longer flew in the area, so we were helped out by the SAM.

My stomach knotted as I thought about getting on the little plane. We weighed in—ourselves and our luggage—to make sure we were within the plane's capability. I had no reason to worry. The flight into Tobité was smooth, but I couldn't help thinking of my mother's long treks.

The forty-minute trip turned into an hour and forty minutes. Greg had never flown here, and he was very careful. He did a flyover before we landed to feel the wind and chase away any cows or other animals that might be on the field. The *pista*—the air strip—was rarely used and had been cleared by hand for us.

A tractor and trailer were waiting to take us to where some nationals served as missionaries. Being so short, I had a time getting on the trailer, but the men put the tailgate down and helped me. Planes coming into the area always attracted a crowd, and this time was no different. A group of children followed us on our tractor pull, and they laughed when I couldn't keep my balance as we bumped along.

We soon arrived at the home of the NTM missionaries now serving here and sat down for a visit with the nationals who now served alongside our representatives. These were the ones who headed up the AWANA program in that part of the country. One of the leaders, Abram, asked if I would like to go into the village to meet some of the Ayorés. Our time was limited here, and we weren't sure about walking that far, but I was willing to try. As we stepped outside, a group of Ayorés—men, women, and children—sat quietly in front of the house. They'd heard we were coming.

They were as happy to see us as we were to see them. Communication came quickly and easily. I'd brought pictures from when Ron's family had lived there, and some of the Ayorés recognized them. They chattered on, reminiscing with us. The ladies brought out lovely handmade string bags for us to buy. We had to explain that we couldn't buy them all, but we each bought one.

One of the elders of the tribe, a man named Dihaide, said that he remembered me. It had been forty-three years, but he mentioned the tall fellow with light hair. That would have been Rollie.

Then he told me that his grandfather was with the group that killed our five men. He stressed that he wasn't a part of it. He told me the whole story. I told him I didn't have any hard feelings. His life—the life of his tribe—had been met by the grace of God. For that, my father lost his life. As he'd said so long ago, "By life or by death, whichever brought glory to God."

There I was, witnessing the glory of God.

We had such a grand time with the Ayorés. We took their pictures and then showed them the pictures in the camera, much to their surprise and amusement. Too soon, it was time to go.

Greg had been called to another town, Santo Corazón, to pick up a pregnant woman in trouble. I so wanted to go—it was the last place Mom had seen my father. However, the flight plans were changed and we went to Roboré instead. But I wasn't too disappointed. I was headed for the town where I was born.

Greg left us at the airstrip in Roboré, and Richelle, Donna, and I took a cab into town. There was only one hotel—a square building with the courtyard in the middle. This was the very building where my mother had lived with the other missionaries, where she'd waited for my birth, where I surprised her by coming early. This was the place of my birth.

The Hotel Pacheco had become a nice little place for visitors to stay, run by a family who lived in town when my parents were there so many years ago. The one lady who remembered Mom and Dad was out of town and I was sorry to miss her. But I was thrilled to be there, a place that was part of my personal history. We had one of the best rooms in the hotel, complete with a TV, air conditioner, ceiling fan, and a private bathroom.

However, TV reception was not available. We couldn't reach the switch for the air conditioner. Of the two beds, one was a board on legs with a very thin mattress; the other had springs and sagged badly in the middle. The hammocks Mom slept in might have been better. No hot water—we took cold showers. But Mom would have been so happy with the one thing she always wanted. Indoor plumbing had finally arrived in Bolivia.

Despite its lacking, the place was clean and we felt safe there. We rested for a while, then set out to find a couple that some missionary friends told us to look up. Maria and Ignacio were so sweet. She served us *cafecitas*—little coffees. We looked at photos as they told us about their lives in Bolivia. Their church was small, but grounded in the Word. The first missionaries had taught them well, he said.

"Do you mean the missionaries who came in 1943?" I asked.

"Yes," he said. "The same ones."

My heart filled with love and emotion. The work of the Lord was carrying on. The seeds planted by my parents and the others had found good ground.

I took in the atmosphere of the wonderful little town. The army base. The dirt streets. The central square. There were three churches. We were careful what we ate. I liked Bolivian food, but it no longer liked me. And not every place serving food met even the most basic of regulations. We waited for our pilot Greg to return and tell us where to go, and where not to go. The bathrooms in town had little baskets in which to deposit our used toilet paper. Once, we even had to pay for the paper. But none of that deterred us from the experience. As we prepared to leave on Sunday morning, Richelle and I took a last walk outside. We saw what we thought were statues of two donkeys. But soon they twitched their tails. Someone had parked their donkeys right in the town square.

"Let's just sit on the park bench and listen to the pretty music coming from the Catholic church," I told Richelle. There couldn't have been a more perfect time for me to be there—it was Father's Day. I breathed in the air and enjoyed the blue sky. I'd always remember the peace and beauty of Sunday morning in Roboré.

We hadn't attended services at one of the three churches because Greg told us to be at the air strip by nine. A quick breakfast of *empanadas* and tea was provided at the hotel before we left. We said goodbye to the believers as they headed to church, and then made our way to our waiting plane. I couldn't wait for the next stop. We were headed for Tambo.

As with our other flights, I was permitted to act as co-pilot. My headphones allowed communication with Greg during our nearly three hour flight. As we entered the valley where Tambo waited, I looked over the lush greenness of the land with its huge flowering trees. I had never seen this before. The mountains, rivers, and farmlands were glorious. But soon the landscape became high and dry, covered with cactus. Then I saw the white mountain. This was what I remembered.

We landed on the prickly *pista.* The team ran to meet us. A good American meal of burgers, mashed potatoes, and veggies was enjoyed by all. After we ate, I wanted to walk to the famous white mountain where I'd hiked and played "capture the flag" as a child. A company had acquired the land and was digging out the mica to make cleaning products. This was causing the mountain to shrink. A barbed-wire fence surrounded the place, but I was determined to walk up the hill.

Several of the team from the boarding school went with me and we got past the fence. I told stories from my days at the school as we hiked up the side of the white mountain. Next, I wanted to see the river where I swam, where I was baptized. Despite the late hour, we made the hike. We found the area was closed. Another company had taken over the land and was taking out the river rock. But we went upstream a ways and gathered a few rocks for souvenirs.

"Your excitement, Avis, is making this whole trip for us," some said. Now came the bittersweet reality of being here. The boarding school in Tambo was moving. The ladies from the conference who'd gone ahead of us were packing and helping to get the property ready to be sold. The contingency committee had determined the best place for the boarding school was in town. Tambo meant "a place to rest." After all the years in the peaceful land, the political environment made safety a concern. The school was just too far away for help to arrive quickly. A guerrilla or terrorist attack would mean disaster—the school couldn't be evacuated easily.

I joined the team in preparing for the move. How things had changed in the world, in Bolivia, and on this campus. Several staff houses had been added. A gym and recreation center had gone up next to the soccer field. All the dorms had kitchenettes and, wonder of wonders, inside toilets and showers. A brand new chapel with a wonderful stage area was used for events throughout the year. Now it would all be sold.

The boarding school would continue educating missionary kids in its new location. The missionaries of Bolivia would go on with the work that the Lord began in 1943. I could see the fruits of my parents' labor everywhere I went on this journey.

I could see my father, a smile on his face and a light in his heart as he walked into the dense green jungle, where he laid down his life for the sake of bringing the Good News to a people who had not heard.

> *"I will both lie down in peace, and sleep; For You alone, O Lord, make me dwell in safety"* (Psalm 4:8).

CONCLUSION

Ron and I recently celebrated our fiftieth wedding anniversary. Friends gathered with us in celebration. Our children cooked and decorated for the party. We shared a slide show of our lives together. Guests used paper and supplies placed on each table to create special cards for us. What a wonderful day. Fifty years spent with the man I love. We struggled at times, but God blessed us.

Just a few months after our party Ron became ill. On January 30, 2014 he went home, where he met David Bacon, the father I never knew. Tears were not without celebration. Heartache didn't subdue God's peace.

Recollection came with pictures and stories. I relived every moment. Along with the memories of my life with Ron came the realization that God had brought me through so much. My father met the jungle sure of his calling, completely abandoned to God's will. Life, I discovered, is filled with all kinds of jungles. At times I found myself less sure of God's calling. Less certain that I possessed such absolute dedication.

At the time I became a wife and mother, I still had in my mind and heart that the Christian life required great toil. I looked up to the missionaries who, like my parents, gave of their time and money, even gave their lives completely. I wanted to please God, but working so hard to keep the rules kept me from knowing that God truly loved me. My effort, my heritage, my father's sacrifice didn't make a difference in how God viewed me. My *Heavenly* Father's sacrifice was what mattered. When God saw me, He saw one redeemed by the blood of His Son.

Now I know that I'm made for His glory, accepted, saved for eternity to reign with Him. I don't have to try to please Him—I can simply rest in His grace. My past, present, and future are His. Living for Jesus, by the power of the Holy Spirit, means that Jesus lives through me. No amount of fretting about my unworthiness will help. I don't have to beg God to forgive me. He already did. I've learned that a grateful heart doesn't wallow in worry and shame.

At times, my heart still fails to trust Him. But He gave me the Comforter to teach me, encourage me, and fill me with God's love. At times I've been judgmental, blamed others for my problems, and grown impatient waiting for God to work in my life.

His patience with me has never failed. For that I thank Him. Blessings and trials I will meet by His providence. I am forever in His hands.

Read at Ron's memorial service:

> For I know that this will turn out for my deliverance through your prayer and the supply of the Spirit of Jesus Christ, according to my earnest expectation and hope that in nothing I shall be ashamed, but with all boldness, as always, so now also Christ will be magnified in my body, whether by life or by death. For to me, to live is Christ, and to die is gain. But if *I* live on in the flesh, this will mean fruit from my labor; yet what I shall choose I cannot tell. For I am hard-pressed between the two, having a desire to depart and be with Christ,

which is far better. Nevertheless to remain in the flesh is more needful for you. And being confident of this, I know that I shall remain and continue with you all for your progress and joy of faith, that your rejoicing for me may be more abundant in Jesus Christ by my coming to you again.

Resources used in writing this book:

God Planted Five Seeds Jean Dye Johnson, New Tribes Mission 1966

The personal writings of Audrey Burgess Bacon Hoogshagen

GLOSSARY

Aríca, Chili – port city in Northern Chile where the group caught the train to Bolivia

Ayoré – unreached people group living in the jungles

Beni or El Beni – northeastern department of Bolivia in the lowlands region of the country

Cochabamba – city in Central Bolivia in a valley of the Andes mountain range

Corumbá, Brazil – city on the Paraguay River in southwestern Brazil

Dihaide – elder of the tribe in 2004

El Carmen – a small town in Santa Cruz department

Eugenia – wife of the Piaroa chief

Doctor Pacheco – attending physician at Avis' birth

Dupáde – the Ayoré word for God

Ese Éjja – people group mom worked with in the Beni

La Paz – highest administrative capital in the world, resting on the Andes altiplano plateau at 11,942 feet above sea level

Manapiare – tributary off of the Ventuari , which flows southwest to the Orinoco River

Piaroa – people group of the middle Orinoco river basin in Venezuela

Pista – runway, airstrip

Porton – a railroad town in Santa Cruz department on the way to the Ayoré

Raphael – chief of the Piaroas

Roboré – military town in Eastern Bolivia

Santa Corazon – town situated in Santa Cruz department

Santa Cruz – capital of Santa Cruz department in the lowlands east of the Andes mountain range

Santa Rosa – a small town in the Amazon pampas of the Beni department

Santiago – rural town in the Beni Department of Bolivia

Tobité – locality within Santa Cruz where the Ayoré work was based

ABOUT THE AUTHOR

Avis grew up in Bolivia, where her mother served as a missionary for New Tribes Mission. After moving to the United States as a young woman, Avis married Ron Bodin. They served in Venezuela before returning to serve in the capacity of administrators in Sanford, Florida.

They remained and served at the international headquarters of NTM until they retired in 2007.

Ron passed away in 2014. Avis still lives in the NTM retirement community in Sanford.

CPSIA information can be obtained
at www.ICGtesting.com
Printed in the USA
BVHW040951160220
572482BV00019B/1157